Battle Orders • 29

The British Army on the Western Front 1916

Bruce I Gudmundsson

Consultant Editor Dr Duncan Anderson • *Series editors* Marcus Cowper and Nikolai Bogdanovic

First published in Great Britain in 2007 by Osprey Publishing
Midland House, West Way, Botley, Oxford OX2 0PH, United Kingdom
443 Park Avenue South, New York, NY 10016, USA
Email: info@ospreypublishing.com

ISBN 978 184603 111 3

Editorial by Ilios Publishing, Oxford, UK (www.iliospublishing.com)
Page layout by Boundford.com, Huntingdon. UK
Index by Glyn Sutcliffe
Typeset in GillSans and Stone Serif
Originated by United Graphics, Singapore
Printed in China through Bookbuilders

07 08 09 10 11   10 9 8 7 6 5 4 3 2 1

A CIP catalogue record for this book is available from the British Library.

For a catalogue of all books published by Osprey Military and Aviation please contact:

Osprey Direct UK, P.O. Box 140, Wellingborough, Northants, NN8 2FA, UK
E-mail: info@ospreydirect.co.uk

Osprey Direct USA, c/o Random House Distribution Center, 400 Hahn Rd,
Westminster, MD 21157 USA
E-mail: info@ospreydirect.com

www.ospreypublishing.com

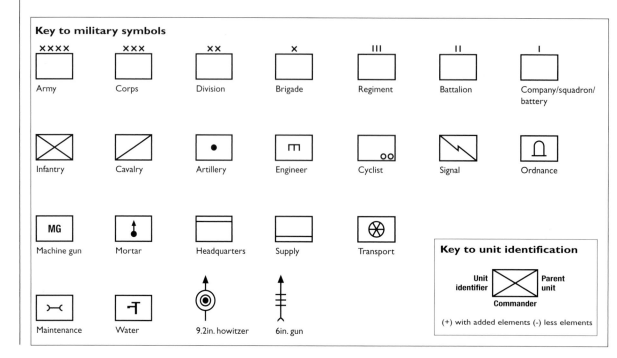

Key to military symbols

××××	×××	××	×	III	II	I
Army	Corps	Division	Brigade	Regiment	Battalion	Company/squadron/battery

Infantry	Cavalry	Artillery	Engineer	Cyclist	Signal	Ordnance

MG				
Machine gun	Mortar	Headquarters	Supply	Transport

Key to unit identification

Unit identifier — Parent unit — Commander

(+) with added elements (-) less elements

Maintenance	Water	9.2in. howitzer	6in. gun

Contents

Introduction

The end of the first year of World War I found the British Empire and its allies in a difficult position. On the Eastern Front, the Germans had inflicted a series of stinging defeats upon the Russians. In the course of doing this, they had eliminated the danger to their own territories in the east, greatly reduced the pressure on the Austria-Hungarian position in the Carpathian Mountains, and conquered nearly all of Russian Poland. In the Mediterranean, the Anglo-French landings on both sides of the Dardanelles had resulted in the same sort of trench warfare that had earlier set in on the Western Front. Along the Alpine

1915 had been a good year for the Central Powers. In addition to maintaining their position in France, they conquered most of Russian Poland, a substantial portion of Baltic littoral and all of Serbia. This French poster advertises an exhibition held to raise money for the relief of Serbian refugees. (Library of Congress)

4

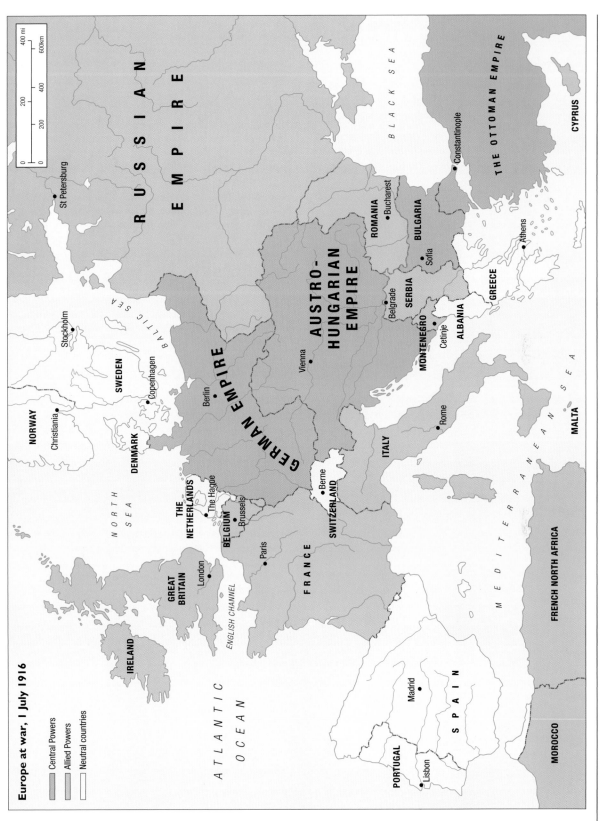

Europe at war, 1 July 1916

Central Powers
Allied Powers
Neutral countries

400 mi
600km

RUSSIAN EMPIRE

THE OTTOMAN EMPIRE

CYPRUS

BLACK SEA

St Petersburg

Constantinople

ROMANIA
• Bucharest

BULGARIA

• Sofia

GREECE

SERBIA

Athens

• Belgrade

MONTENEGRO

ALBANIA

AUSTRO-HUNGARIAN EMPIRE

• Cetinje

Stockholm

SWEDEN

• Copenhagen

• Vienna

BALTIC SEA

Berlin

GERMAN EMPIRE

• Rome

MEDITERRANEAN SEA

NORWAY

• Christiania

DENMARK

ITALY

MALTA

• Berne

SWITZERLAND

THE NETHERLANDS

• The Hague

• Brussels

BELGIUM

NORTH SEA

FRANCE

• Paris

FRENCH NORTH AFRICA

GREAT BRITAIN

• London

ENGLISH CHANNEL

IRELAND

ATLANTIC OCEAN

SPAIN

• Madrid

PORTUGAL

• Lisbon

MOROCCO

During the first two years of World War I, two European states (Italy and Romania) entered the war on the side of the Allies and two (Bulgaria and the Ottoman Empire) joined the Central Powers.

Sir John French (1852–1925) who had taken command of the Expeditionary Force at the very start of the war, was relieved of that position on 19 December 1915. (Library of Congress)

border of Austria-Hungary, the long-awaited entry of the Italian Army into the fray had done little to tip the balance in favour of the anti-German alliance. On the Western Front itself, the many small-scale offensives carried out by Allied forces had failed to achieve their primary objective – tying down so many Germans in the west that they would be powerless to take the offensive on other fronts. Indeed, as the first year of the war came to a close, the Germans were laying the groundwork for the offensive that would, quite literally, drive the field armies of Serbia into the sea.

As ominous as it was, the dark cloud that hung over the British Empire was not without a silver lining. The Royal Navy controlled the great oceans, giving the Allied nations full access to the resources of the world outside of Europe while denying them to the Central Powers. The British Army was still expanding, and so new divisions were made available to the Expeditionary Force at an unprecedented rate. (At the start of 1916, these would be joined by the dozens of divisions made available by the withdrawal of British Empire forces from the Dardanelles.) Newly forged weapons were beginning to emerge from British factories, while the enormous industrial and agricultural capacity of North America was being harnessed to provide those weapons with the horses, mules and tractors they needed to be useful on the battlefield. What was even more important, the truly gargantuan quantities of ammunition needed by these weapons were about to become available, to the point where the very definitions of such things as 'shell rationing' and 'intense bombardment' were beginning to change.

Closer to the front, the Expeditionary Force itself was innovating at a furious pace. Weapons, techniques and concepts that had barely been imagined before the outbreak of the war – such things as poison gas, underground warfare and aerial combat – were becoming part of its daily reality. The advent of trench mortars, hand grenades, rifle grenades, and light machine guns held out the promise of a near future in which infantry units would wield unprecedented firepower. At the same time, the hundreds of heavy artillery batteries being formed for service in France and Flanders gave hope to those who believed that the only road to victory was one paved with howitzer shells. The innovation that mattered most, however, was not yet on the horizon. That was the creation of the institutions, techniques and attitudes needed to translate the enormous vitality, ingenuity and firepower placed at the disposition of the Expeditionary Force into unqualified battlefield success.

Mission

At the start of the second year of World War I, the Expeditionary Force had two great tasks to accomplish. The first was to finish the job of converting itself into a large, powerful and thoroughly modern army – one that could help the French Army to strike a decisive, war-winning blow against the German forces in the west. The second was to prevent any of the other Allied powers – whether Russia, Italy, Serbia, or even France – from concluding a separate peace with Germany. Unfortunately, these two tasks were very much at odds with each other. The first required the careful husbanding of forces, as well as a gargantuan effort to build up the infrastructure of schools, depots, rest camps, bakeries, butcheries, workshops, warehouses, hospitals, railways, aerodromes, ammunition dumps and headquarters needed to keep such an army in fighting trim. The second required aggressive offensive enterprises, attacks on a scale large enough to create the possibility of a substantial penetration of the German front line. These were necessary, not merely to tie down the largest possible number of German divisions, but also to prove to the governments and people of Allied countries that the British Empire was as willing as they were to sacrifice its sons for the sake of the common cause.

Neither the expansion of the Expeditionary Force nor the offensives launched in support of the French and Russian armies were, however, ends in themselves. In the minds of Allied strategists, both served the larger purpose of setting the stage for a series of large-scale offensives that would, at the very least, drive the Germans out of much of the French and Belgian territory that they had conquered in 1914. As the French Army had already exhausted every significant source of military manpower, both French and British leaders agreed that the Expeditionary Force would provide the lion's share of the forces taking part in these offensives.

With this in mind, the Expeditionary Force began to assemble a powerful operational reserve behind the Western Front. Consisting of recently formed divisions that had just crossed the English Channel, divisions transferred from the Middle East, and divisions withdrawn from front-line service, this reserve was to give the British leadership the ability to launch its first offensive at some point in the spring or summer of 1916. Until that time, it served the secondary purpose of allowing new divisions to complete their training and exhausted ones to rest.

On 21 February 1916, the German offensive in the vicinity of Verdun put a halt to British plans for a massive spring offensive. Instead of building up their strength for the great push, the divisions of the operational reserve were sent forward to take responsibility for defensive positions that had previously been held by French formations. At the same time, the British leadership began planning a very different sort of offensive – one designed to relieve pressure on the hard-pressed French Army rather than drive the Germans out of a substantial piece of French territory. This offensive, which began on 1 July 1916, was the famous battle of the Somme.

Sir Douglas Haig (1861–1928), who had commanded the First Army for most of 1915, took command of the entire Expeditionary Force on 19 December 1915. (Library of Congress)

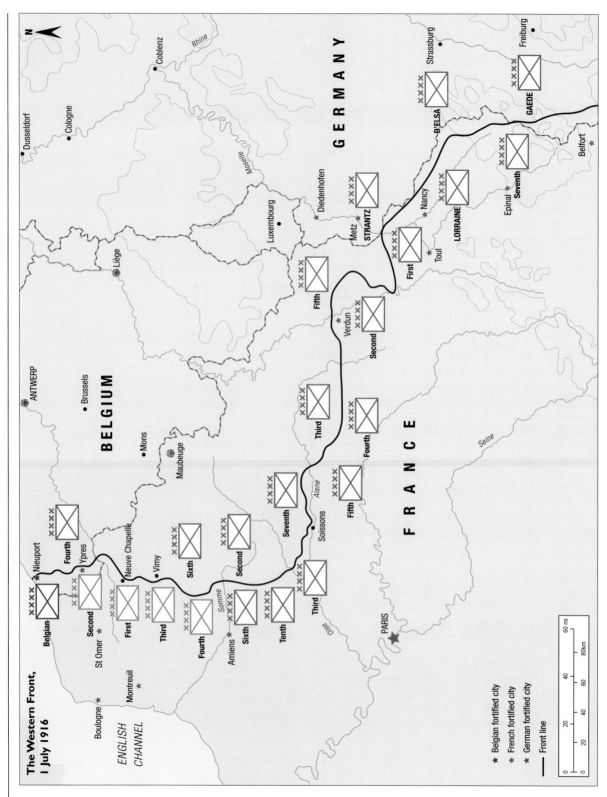

The Western Front,
1 July 1916

The great scar cut across the face of Europe by the onset of positional warfare in the autumn of 1914 would not shift significantly until the spring of 1917. Nonetheless, the second year of World War I saw significant changes on both sides of no man's land. On the German side, this was largely a matter of the thinning out of defensive garrisons in order to provide troops for the Eastern Front. On the Allied side, the portion of the Western Front held by British forces expanded while that held by French formations shrank.

Growth of the Expeditionary Force

On 5 August 1915, the first anniversary of the decision to send the Expeditionary Force to France, British Empire forces on the Western Front included 27 infantry divisions, five cavalry divisions and a bewildering array of non-divisional units. The latter included 32 heavy batteries, 23 siege batteries, 23 anti-aircraft sections, and 46 engineer companies that specialized in work ranging from the operation of railways and the printing of maps to the digging of tunnels and the delivery of poison gas. A year later, on 5 August 1916, the number of infantry divisions had risen to 55 and the number of heavy batteries to 62. The greatest growth within the Expeditionary Force, however, took place in those non-divisional units that were particularly useful in trench warfare. Thus, while the number of infantry divisions increased by a factor of two, the number of specialized engineer companies grew by a factor of eight (from 46 to 340), the number of siege batteries by a factor of six (from 23 to 132) and the number of trench mortar batteries by a factor of ten (from 35 to more than 350).

The most important sources of infantry divisions for the Expeditionary Force in the second year of the war were the Third, Fourth and Fifth New

Table 1: Officers and men serving with the British Expeditionary Force	
Date	Number
15 September 1914	163,897
31 January 1915	347,384
31 May 1915	601,000
24 August 1915	858,825
1 January 1916	987,200
1 April 1916	1,146,357
1 August 1916	1,483,915
1 October 1916	1,546,474
1 January 1917	1,581,745

2   LE MIROIR

DANS LES TRANCHÉES DE LA ROUTE D'YPRES

SOLDATS ANGLAIS ATTENDANT L'HEURE DE LA RELÈVE DANS LEURS TAUPINIÈRES .

Le sol de la vieille Flandre est partout coupé de tranchées profondes où se tiennent perpétuellement sur le qui-vive des combattants que nulle fatigue ne peut abattre. La plus franche gaieté règne dans ces trous que l'ingéniosité des soldats réussit à rendre presque confor- tables. Alors que les Allemands sont dévorés par la vermine, les alliés observent les lois de l'hygiène et se construisent jusqu'à des bains-douches. Les Anglais surtout sont étonnants, rasés de frais, propres et nets comme s'ils étaient arrivés la veille de la caserne.

Members of the Expeditionary Force got their first taste of trench warfare in September 1914, when they dug temporary positions such as these along the line of the river Aisne. (Great War in a Different Light)

Armies. Together, these three series of entirely new divisions provided 14 of the 30 infantry divisions that reported for duty on the Western Front between 5 August 1915 and 5 August 1916. The second most important source of infantry divisions during this period was the 'Imperial Strategic Reserve' of infantry divisions that had been formed in Egypt in the winter of 1916. This reservoir of formations, which was created on the framework provided by the forces that had served in the Gallipoli campaign, provided seven divisions to the Expeditionary Force. (Five of these divisions – the New Zealand Division and four Australian divisions – were from the Antipodes. The other two divisions were composed mostly of units of the British Army.)

The remainder of the divisions that joined the Expeditionary Force in the eleven months that preceded the battle of the Somme came from a variety of sources. Four – the Guards Division, the 16th (Irish) Division and two Territorial Force divisions – were assembled from various pre-existing elements. (Most of this assembly took place in France. The 16th Division, however, was put together in the United Kingdom before crossing the English Channel.) Two were recently formed Canadian divisions. One was the Royal Naval Division. The last two, a harbinger of things to come, were Territorial Force divisions composed mostly of second-line units. These units, which had originally been formed as home defence units, had been made available for overseas service by the same Military Service Act that introduced conscription.

Table 2: Infantry divisions joining the Expeditionary Force, August 1914–July 1916

Type of Division	Divisions	Dates
Original Expeditionary Force	1st, 2nd, 3rd, 4th, 5th and 6th	August 1914 to September 1914
Improvised Regular	Meerut*, Lahore*, 7th, 8th, 27th* and 28th*	October 1914 to January 1915
Canadian	1st Canadian, 2nd Canadian and 3rd Canadian	February 1915 to December 1915
Territorial Force	46th, 47th, 48th, 49th, 50th and 51st	March 1915 to May 1915
First New Army (K1)	9th, 12th and 14th	May 1915
Second New Army (K2)	15th, 17th, 18th, 19th and 20th	July 1915
Guards Division	Guards	August 1915
Third New Army (K3)	21st, 22nd*, 23rd, 24th, 25th and 26th*	August 1915 to October 1915
Fourth New Army (K4)	30th, 31st, 32nd, 33rd, 34th and 35th	November 1915 to February 1916
Reconstituted Divisions	16th, 55th and 56th	January 1916 to February 1916
Fifth New Army (K5)	36th, 37th, 38th, 39th, 40th and 41st	July 1915 to June 1916
'Imperial Reserve' (Egypt)	New Zealand, 1st Australian, 2nd Australian, 4th Australian, 5th Australian, 11th and 29th	March 1916 to June 1916
Royal Naval Division	63rd	May 1916
Territorial Force (Second Line)	60th and 61st	May 1916 to June 1916

Divisions marked with an asterisk (*) left the Western Front between 5 August 1915 and 31 December 1915.

Doctrine and training

The British Army of the 19th century had very little in the way of formal doctrine. Indeed, many British officers of those years viewed doctrine as a foreign concept that had little relevance to a force that existed to fight a wide variety of enemies in a wide variety of environments. In such an army, these officers argued, the only knowledge of value was local knowledge. For much the same reason, most of the training conducted by the British Army was of the 'on-the-job' variety. That is, British soldiers did most of their learning in an ad hoc manner, with service in operational units taking the place of training establishments and the advice or example of more experienced comrades doing the work that would later be reserved for well-defined programmes of instruction.

In the years after the Boer War (1899–1902), this system of informal apprenticeship began to break down. The chief reason for this was a shift in strategic priorities. The British Army of the late 19th century was theoretically capable of forming its far-flung garrisons into a field army of the European type. Its principal business, however, was imperial defence. In the early years of the 20th century, the ability to conduct the many small wars required to maintain 'dominion over palm and pine' was increasingly seen as a by-product of the ability to wage war on a much grander scale. This larger ability, in turn, was seen to depend upon a large number of units trained to a predictable, repeatable standard rather than a small number of men with an intimate knowledge of local conditions. Because of this, the decade that preceded the outbreak of World War I saw a great increase in the number of formal training programmes, specialized training units and universally applicable training manuals. The exception that proves this rule is the Royal Garrison Artillery. Composed mostly of units that had been closely tailored to the requirements of particular fortifications, this branch continued to conduct the bulk of its training – including the initial training of new recruits – in operational coastal defence units.

The events of the first few months of World War I had the paradoxical effect of turning back the clock on both training methods and doctrine. The raising of the New Armies and the great expansion of the Territorial Force, as well as the practice of employing troops in training for various duties related to home defence, caused a revival of the old practice of conducting most training within operational units. However, in contrast to the operational units of the old Regular Army, the units mobilized or formed in the late summer of 1914 were poorly provided with the experienced soldiers and professional non-commissioned officers that made the old system work as well as it had. The result was the employment of a large number of expedients – the employment of policemen and prison warders to teach drill, the hiring of schoolteachers to conduct physical training, and extensive reliance upon the many drill manuals and handbooks produced in the years before the war.

By November 1914, various authorities, both at home and within the Expeditionary Force, had begun to create schools and courses of various kinds. Some of these, such as the scheme to mass-produce siege artillery batteries, trained complete units. Others, such as the courses for shoeing smiths and military cooks, produced individual specialists. Closer to the front, courses in the handling of hand grenades, machine guns and trench mortars helped units adapt to the new reality of trench warfare.

ABOVE A far cry from the recruiting posters of the first year of the war, this notice makes no appeal to honour, ambition or patriotism. Rather, it is little more than an explanation of the rules governing conscription. (Library of Congress)

RIGHT Traditionally, most efforts to attract recruits to the British Army were conducted by individual regiments. This practice, which strengthened attachment to particular units rather than the Army as a whole, continued well into 1915. (Library of Congress)

Mobilization

The men who made possible the growth of the Expeditionary Force in the second year of World War I had, for the most part, enlisted during the first year of the war. By the summer of 1915, the great flood of men who were led to join the British Army by a combination of patriotism, peer pressure and desire for adventure had been reduced to a trickle. The old methods of recruiting, which had relied heavily on the efforts of local communities and individual regiments, were no longer working. Likewise, the old system by which a man joined a particular regiment or corps, rather than the British Army as whole, was making it difficult to keep certain units up to strength. In particular, the fact that members of the Territorial Force could not be sent beyond the borders of the United Kingdom without their express consent had created a manpower crisis in many of the Territorial Force infantry battalions serving on the Western Front.

Beginning in the autumn of 1915, Parliament enacted a series of measures to both rationalize and stimulate military recruitment within the United Kingdom. The first of these was the 'Derby Scheme', which replaced traditional enlistment with a system of 'attestation'. Thus, rather than enlisting directly (and immediately) into a specific regiment or corps, a man simply promised to

As the Expeditionary Force grew, so did the home establishment of the British Army. By the end of 1916, more than a million British soldiers were serving in the British Isles. Of these, 40 per cent were considered 'fit for general service abroad'. The rest were either recovering from wounds or suffering from a permanent condition that prevented them from serving with a fighting unit. (US National Archives)

serve if (and when) he was needed. When combined with an effective publicity campaign and active canvassing by local notables, the Derby Scheme had three important effects. The first was to convince a large number of men to enlist immediately and so join the regiment of their choice while they were still able to exercise that option. The second was to reduce the pain of enlisting for immediate service. That is to say, by declaring himself willing to serve, a man could immediately enjoy many of the social and psychological benefits of enlistment without immediately subjecting himself to the rigours, hardships and risks of military service. The third effect of the Derby Scheme was to put into place a system by which the British Army would only induct men when they were actually required, and thus avoid both the 'feasts' and the 'famines' associated with traditional enlistment.

Though it convinced 200,000 men to enlist directly and two million men to promise to serve if called, the Derby Scheme failed to provide enough men to meet the anticipated needs of the British Army. As a direct result of this, Parliament passed the first Military Service Act. Among other things, this law made all single men of military age subject to conscription, and voided all provisions of enlistment contracts that prevented a soldier from being transferred from any one unit, regiment or corps to any other unit, regiment or corps. The first Military Service Act thus wrought two simultaneous revolutions. The first was the introduction of general conscription for overseas service. The second was a great increase in the homogeneity of the British Army and, by extension, the Expeditionary Force.

Unit organization

During the first year of World War I, the units that the British Army provided to the Expeditionary Force were organized in accordance with three different sets of war establishments. There was one set of war establishments for units of the Regular Army, one for units of the Territorial Force and one for units formed as one of the five New Armies. Because of this, two units of the same basic type were often formed on distinct, and, in some cases, highly divergent, patterns. A Regular Army field artillery battery, for example, was 50 per cent larger than a New Army field artillery battery, while a Territorial field artillery battery was of roughly the same size as its New Army counterpart, but was armed with an entirely different model of field gun or howitzer.

In the course of the second year of World War I, the differences between the three sets of war establishments all but disappeared. (The last units to achieve uniformity were field artillery batteries, some of which retained distinguishing organizational features until January 1917.) As a result, it became far easier to assign units formed by one contingent to formations created by another. That is to say, uniformity of organization did for the Expeditionary Force what standardized manufacture did for rifles – it made each component of a given type fully interchangeable with all other components of that type.

The ability to replace any infantry battalion, cavalry regiment, field gun battery, howitzer battery or engineer field company with another had long been a feature of the Regular Army. Indeed, the 'system of reliefs' – the regular transfer of units between stations in the British Isles and various parts of a global empire – would have been greatly complicated by organizational differences between units of the same type. This sort of modularity, however, was alien to many of the New Army infantry divisions and nearly all of those of the Territorial Force. These formations, like most of those of the German Army, had been based upon the principle of what might, in retrospect, be called 'nested cohesion'. That is to say, the battalions of a given infantry brigade and the batteries of a given field artillery brigade were often drawn from neighbouring communities. These brigades, in turn, were part of divisions with a distinct regional character. Thus, the 137th (Staffordshire) Brigade of the 46th (North Midland) Division drew its four battalions from the relatively large county of Staffordshire. (Two of these battalions were from the South Staffordshire Regiment. Two were from the North Staffordshire Regiment.) The 138th (Lincoln and Leicester) Brigade got its four battalions from the nearby cities of Lincoln and Leicester, as well as from the surrounding countryside. (As might be expected, these battalions were affiliated with either the Lincolnshire Regiment or the Leicestershire Regiment.) The 139th (Sherwood Foresters) Brigade had battalions that hailed from the adjacent counties of Nottinghamshire and Derbyshire. All four of these battalions belonged to the 'county' regiment linked to these two counties – the Sherwood Foresters (Nottinghamshire and Derbyshire Regiment).

In some formations, the system of 'nested cohesion' remained in force throughout the middle period of the war. (The only 'alien' unit to join the aforementioned North Midlands Divisions in 1916, for example, was the 1st Battalion of the Monmouthshire Regiment. This unit, with many miners in its ranks, served as the divisional pioneer battalion.) In other formations, the desire to get the largest number of men into action in the shortest possible time led to situations where the largest organization with any regional character at all was an infantry brigade. In the 39th Division, for example, only one brigade was exclusively linked to a particular locality. (This brigade, the 110th Infantry Brigade, was composed of four battalions of the Leicestershire Regiment.) The other two brigades were nearly as mixed as any brigade of the Regular Army. (Each had two battalions from the same general area and two battalions with no geographical or regimental connection to any other in the division.)

The only formations that managed to increase the degree of 'nested cohesion' that they enjoyed in 1916 were those that came from Canada and Australia. On 15 September 1915, most of the Canadian units on the Western Front were formed into the Canadian Corps. As time went on, this formation grew progressively more Canadian as specialized units, staff officers and formation commanders provided by the British Army were replaced by their Canadian counterparts. In the spring of 1916, the two Australia–New Zealand army corps (I ANZAC and II ANZAC) that had been formed in the Mediterranean theatre joined the Expeditionary Force. After arriving on the Western Front, I ANZAC evolved into an exclusively Australian formation. As Australian divisions, units, staffs and commanders were concentrated in I ANZAC, II ANZAC began to lose much of its distinctly Antipodean character. Thus, in December 1917, when I ANZAC was renamed the Australian Corps, II ANZAC became a numbered army corps of the British Expeditionary Force.

Armies

The Expeditionary Force was originally organized as a small field army, the rough equivalent of the numbered armies of France and Germany. By Christmas 1914, however, the Expeditionary Force was nearly twice as large as it had been at the start of the war. It was therefore divided, on 26 December 1914, into two numbered armies, the First Army of Sir Douglas Haig and the Second Army of Sir Horace Smith-Dorrien. After that point, a new numbered army was created for every 15 or so new infantry divisions that joined the Expeditionary Force. Thus, the arrival of 15 infantry divisions during the first half of 1915 led to the formation of the Third Army. Likewise, the net gain of 16 infantry divisions that took place between July 1915 and February 1916 prompted the creation of the Fourth Army, and the subsequent appearance of 14 additional infantry divisions in the spring and summer of 1915 led eventually to the establishment of the Fifth Army.

(The Fifth Army began its existence as the Reserve Army. Formed on 23 May 1916, this was a temporary organization that was formed as a means of exploiting any rupture in the German lines that might result from the upcoming Somme offensive. When this breakthrough failed to materialize, the Reserve Army became a sort of 'fire brigade' for the Expeditionary Force as a whole, a means of quickly reinforcing a numbered army that found itself in a particularly difficult position.)

Table 3: Formation of numbered armies, 1914–16			
	Strength of the Expeditionary Force		
Army	Date of formation	Army corps	Infantry divisions
First and Second	26 December 1914	6	12
Third	18 July 1915	9	27
Fourth	18 March 1916	14	43
Fifth	30 October 1916	18	55

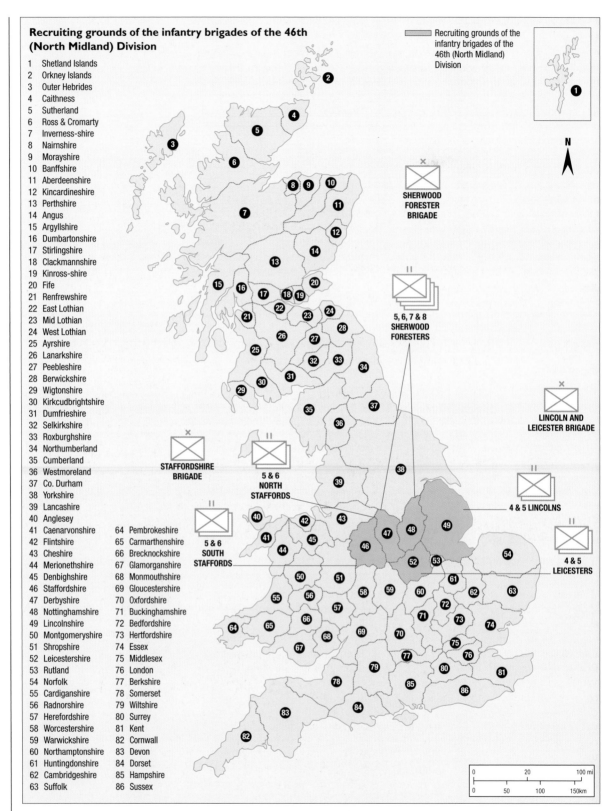

Recruiting grounds of the infantry brigades of the 46th (North Midland) Division

Recruiting grounds of the infantry brigades of the 46th (North Midland) Division

1   Shetland Islands
2   Orkney Islands
3   Outer Hebrides
4   Caithness
5   Sutherland
6   Ross & Cromarty
7   Inverness-shire
8   Nairnshire
9   Morayshire
10 Banffshire
11 Aberdeenshire
12 Kincardineshire
13 Perthshire
14 Angus
15 Argyllshire
16 Dumbartonshire
17 Stirlingshire
18 Clackmannanshire
19 Kinross-shire
20 Fife
21 Renfrewshire
22 East Lothian
23 Mid Lothian
24 West Lothian
25 Ayrshire
26 Lanarkshire
27 Peebleshire
28 Berwickshire
29 Wigtonshire
30 Kirkcudbrightshire
31 Dumfrieshire
32 Selkirkshire
33 Roxburghshire
34 Northumberland
35 Cumberland
36 Westmoreland
37 Co. Durham
38 Yorkshire
39 Lancashire
40 Anglesey
41 Caernarvonshire
42 Flintshire
43 Cheshire
44 Merionethshire
45 Denbighshire
46 Staffordshire
47 Derbyshire
48 Nottinghamshire
49 Lincolnshire
50 Montgomeryshire
51 Shropshire
52 Leicestershire
53 Rutland
54 Norfolk
55 Cardiganshire
56 Radnorshire
57 Herefordshire
58 Worcestershire
59 Warwickshire
60 Northamptonshire
61 Huntingdonshire
62 Cambridgeshire
63 Suffolk
64 Pembrokeshire
65 Carmarthenshire
66 Brecknockshire
67 Glamorganshire
68 Monmouthshire
69 Gloucestershire
70 Oxfordshire
71 Buckinghamshire
72 Bedfordshire
73 Hertfordshire
74 Essex
75 Middlesex
76 London
77 Berkshire
78 Somerset
79 Wiltshire
80 Surrey
81 Kent
82 Cornwall
83 Devon
84 Dorset
85 Hampshire
86 Sussex

SHERWOOD FORESTER BRIGADE

5, 6, 7 & 8 SHERWOOD FORESTERS

LINCOLN AND LEICESTER BRIGADE

STAFFORDSHIRE BRIGADE

5 & 6 NORTH STAFFORDS

4 & 5 LINCOLNS

5 & 6 SOUTH STAFFORDS

4 & 5 LEICESTERS

The 46th Infantry Division, which began the war as the North Midland Division of the Territorial Force, provides an excellent example of 'nested cohesion'. Each infantry battalion was associated with a particular county, each infantry brigade with a pair of counties, and the division as a whole with five neighbouring counties. (Staffordshire, which had a relatively large population, was able to support an entire brigade.)

Army corps

The army corps of the British Army of World War I were an artefact of the decision, taken at the very start of the war, to deploy the original Expeditionary Force on the left wing of the French field armies deployed on the Western Front. Prior to that decision, most of the functions that were performed by army corps in the French and German armies were either performed by divisions or by an intermediate echelon of command known as the 'army (group of two or more divisions)'. This latter echelon, which was more of a temporary task force than a permanent formation, was larger than most contemporary army corps of the day but smaller than most contemporary field armies. For purposes of mobilization, pre-war plans allotted each 'army' three infantry divisions. The records left by pre-war exercises make it clear, however, that once active operations began, the composition of an army would vary considerably, with infantry divisions, the cavalry division and independent cavalry brigades being attached and detached as the operational situation changed.

Table 4: Army corps of the British Army, 1 July 1916			
Army corps	**Date of formation**	**Location at formation**	**Location on 1 July 1916**
I	5 August 1914	Expeditionary Force	Expeditionary Force
II	5 August 1914	Expeditionary Force	Expeditionary Force
III	5 August 1914	Expeditionary Force	Expeditionary Force
IV	9 October 1914	Expeditionary Force	Expeditionary Force
V	18 February 1915	Expeditionary Force	Expeditionary Force
VI	1 June 1915	Expeditionary Force	Expeditionary Force
VII	14 July 1915	Expeditionary Force	Expeditionary Force
VIII	March 1916	Mediterranean	Expeditionary Force
IX	June 1916	United Kingdom	Expeditionary Force
X	14 July 1915	Expeditionary Force	Expeditionary Force
XI	29 August 1915	Expeditionary Force	Expeditionary Force
XII	6 September 1915	Expeditionary Force	Mediterranean
XIII	15 November 1915	Expeditionary Force	Expeditionary Force
XIV	3 January 1916	Expeditionary Force	Expeditionary Force
XV	12 January 1916	Mediterranean	Expeditionary Force
XVI	17 January 1916	Mediterranean	Mediterranean
XVII	9 January 1916	Expeditionary Force	Expeditionary Force

Because the army corps was such a novelty for the British Army, it took some time to sort out the exact role it would play within the Expeditionary Force. The first model that presented itself was that of the French two-division army corps. While that structure had provided the original impetus for the creation of army corps within the Expeditionary Force, it was ill suited to the British tradition of division-centric command. In particular, the commanders of French army corps were accustomed to participating directly in battle. To that end, they were not only provided with a significant number of non-divisional infantry and artillery units, but were also in the habit of micro-managing the commanders of their divisions. (Even in fast-moving situations, the orders issued by French corps commanders to their divisional commanders often gave instructions as to the placement of specific brigades, regiments and even battalions.)

In the spring of 1915, a happy accident suggested a better solution to the problem of how best to organize the army corps of the Expeditionary Force. The six Territorial Force infantry divisions that crossed the English Channel

Infantry establishments of German and British army corps, 1915–17

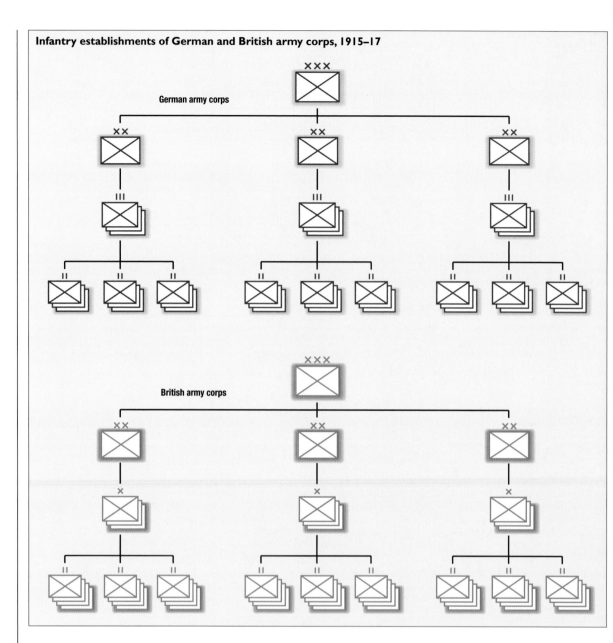

that season had arrived on the Western Front as independent formations. Rather than forming a new army corps for each pair of Territorial Force divisions, these divisions were each assigned to one of the six existing army corps of the Expeditionary Force. This act transformed those army corps from two-division ('binary') formations into three-division ('triangular') ones. It is interesting to note that the German Army also triangularized its army corps in the spring of 1915. The rationale behind this reform, however, was quite different from that which motivated the triangularization of the army corps of the Expeditionary Force. Whereas the leadership of the Expeditionary Force triangularized British army corps in order to accommodate an increase in the number of available divisions, the leadership of the German Army triangularized German army corps on the Western Front in order to create a larger number of somewhat smaller divisions. The British triangularization scheme resulted in a net gain of 12 infantry battalions and 44 artillery pieces for each army corps of the Expeditionary Force. The German triangularization

Infantry and field artillery of the expanded army corps proposed by Sir John French, 4 January 1915

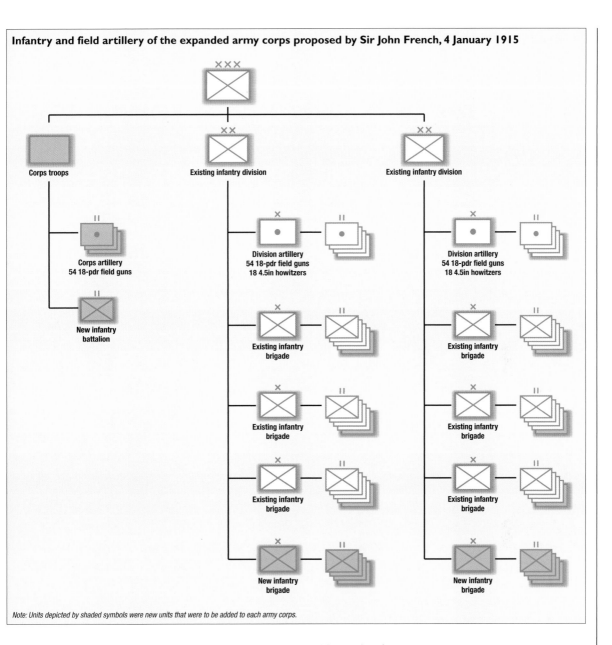

Note: Units depicted by shaded symbols were new units that were to be added to each army corps.

scheme gave each participating army corps only three additional infantry battalions. At the same time, each German army corps taking part in the reorganization lost, on average, two field pieces.

Though it may have started out as a temporary expedient, the triangularization of army corps became a permanent feature of the organizational structure of the Expeditionary Force. One reason for this was the continuing desire to 'season' newly arrived divisions, particularly the many New Army divisions that arrived on the Western Front during the second year of the war. An army corps that possessed two experienced divisions and one newly arrived one could do this by temporarily attaching elements of the newly arrived division to their opposite numbers in experienced divisions. Another argument in favour of the triangular army corps was the chronic shortage of trained staff officers that plagued the British Army during the early years of World War I. This shortage was one of the many by-products of the fact that the British Army of the years prior to

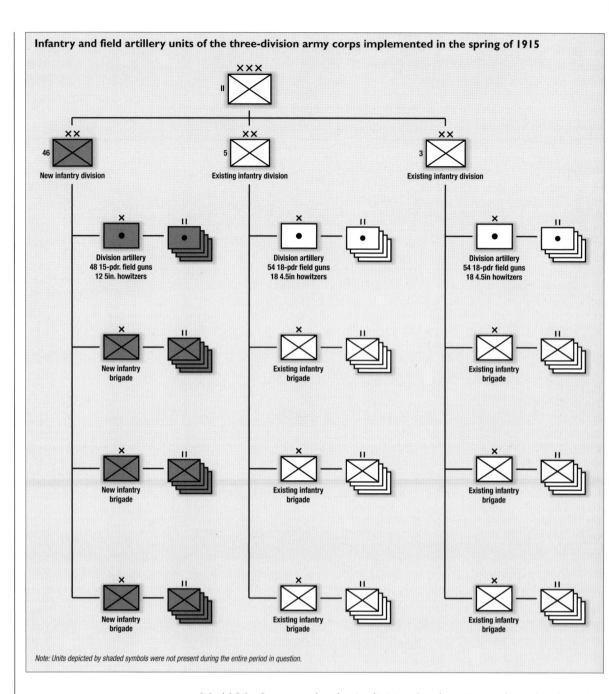

Infantry and field artillery units of the three-division army corps implemented in the spring of 1915

46 — New infantry division

5 — Existing infantry division

3 — Existing infantry division

Division artillery
48 15-pdr. field guns
12 5in. howitzers

Division artillery
54 18-pdr field guns
18 4.5in howitzers

Division artillery
54 18-pdr field guns
18 4.5in howitzers

New infantry brigade

New infantry brigade

New infantry brigade

Existing infantry brigade

Existing infantry brigade

Existing infantry brigade

Existing infantry brigade

Existing infantry brigade

Existing infantry brigade

Note: Units depicted by shaded symbols were not present during the entire period in question.

World War I possessed only six division headquarters and one headquarters of a formation larger than a division.

As early as the first winter of the war, the senior leadership of the British Army began looking for ways to increase the size of the Expeditionary Force without putting any additional strain on the supply of trained staff officers. On 4 January 1915, Sir John French sent a formal memorandum to the War Office laying out his solution to this problem. Rather than form new army corps to accommodate the new divisions being formed for the Expeditionary Corps, he argued, the divisions should be broken up. The units made available by the dissolution of these divisions should then be divided among the six British Empire army corps then serving on the Western Front. Specifically, each of the six army corps of the Expeditionary Force should be provided with 15 additional infantry battalions and nine additional field gun batteries. Fourteen of the battalions were to be given, at a rate of seven battalions per division, to each infantry division. The remaining infantry battalion in each army corps was to be assigned directly to the corps headquarters. Within each division, four of the new battalions would be formed into a new infantry brigade. The three remaining new battalions would be parcelled out, at a rate of one battalion per infantry brigade, to the existing infantry brigades.

The War Office responded to French's proposal by pointing out that its implementation would require nothing less than the complete reinvention, not merely of the standard British infantry division, but of the entire system of command and logistics that had been built around it. This, in turn, would require the rewriting of a large number of manuals, the issue of a completely new set of war establishments, and the redesign of a large number of standard procedures. Thus, rather than economizing on the existing supply of staff officers, the adoption of the 19-battalion infantry division would instantly diminish the competence level of the staff officers who had spent several years mastering the existing system. Nonetheless, while the six Territorial Force divisions scheduled to join the Expeditionary Force in the spring of 1915 were completing their training, the War Office sanctioned the practice of attaching spare Territorial Force infantry battalions to existing infantry brigades. As some brigades received two such battalions, this measure had the effect of temporarily adding six or more (and sometimes as many as 12) extra infantry battalions to army corps serving in France and Belgium.

Cavalry corps

The Expeditionary Force began the second year of World War I with two cavalry corps: the Cavalry Corps and the Indian Cavalry Corps. While of equivalent status to army corps, with commanding officers who ranked as lieutenant-generals, these formations were organized and employed in a very different manner. Where each army corps consisted of three or more infantry divisions and a considerable force of corps troops, each cavalry corps possessed two or three cavalry divisions, but very little in the way of corps troops. Where army corps almost always occupied a particular sector of the front, cavalry corps were invariably stationed well behind the lines. As a rule, moreover, each cavalry corps reported directly to the General Headquarters of the Expeditionary Force as a whole and was only assigned to armies for particular operations. In March 1916, the two cavalry corps were disbanded. Seven months later, however, the Cavalry Corps was reconstituted. From that point in time until the end of the war it had the triple mission of serving as the 'mother church' for all cavalry formations serving with the Expeditionary Force, of providing an organizational home for all cavalry divisions not assigned directly to armies and of providing an operational headquarters for groups of cavalry divisions assembled for service in large-scale offensives.

Corps troops, army troops and GHQ troops

In the first few months of the war, all non-divisional units in the Expeditionary Force were classified as 'army troops'. These, which included signals units, logistics units, squadrons of Irish Horse, infantry battalions, engineer units and squadrons of the Royal Flying Corps, were attached either to the General Headquarters of the Expeditionary Force as a whole (GHQ) or the headquarters of an army corps. When, on 26 December 1914, the Expeditionary Force was divided into armies, a number of non-divisional units found themselves assigned to the headquarters of those formations as well. This led to the creation of three types of organizational homes for non-divisional units – 'corps troops' (which were assigned to army corps), 'army troops' (which were assigned to armies) and 'GHQ troops' (which were assigned directly to the General Headquarters of the Expeditionary Force).

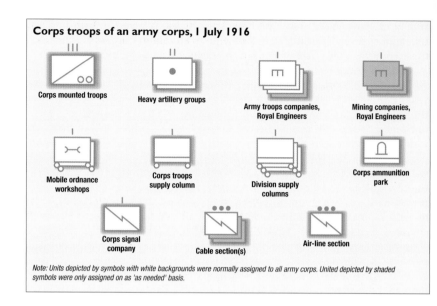

Corps troops of an army corps, 1 July 1916

Corps mounted troops

Heavy artillery groups

Army troops companies, Royal Engineers

Mining companies, Royal Engineers

Mobile ordnance workshops

Corps troops supply column

Division supply columns

Corps ammunition park

Corps signal company

Cable section(s)

Air-line section

Note: Units depicted by symbols with white backgrounds were normally assigned to all army corps. United depicted by shaded symbols were only assigned on as 'as needed' basis.

Some non-divisional units could be found at two or even three different echelons of command. Such was the case with the fortress, siege and tunnelling companies of the Royal Engineers, aeroplane squadrons of the Royal Flying Corps, supply columns of the Army Service Corps and labour companies of various sorts. Other non-divisional units became associated with particular echelons of command. Gas warfare units, camouflage units, meteorology units, printing shops, permanent hospitals, military prisons, prisoner-of-war units and long-distance signals units were, as a rule, assigned to GHQ. Artillery batteries armed with weapons of the heaviest sort (15in. howitzers, 12in. howitzers, 9.2in. howitzers, 8in. howitzers and 6in. guns) were usually assigned to armies. Units concerned with the more demanding kinds of equipment repair, the supply of petrol, and engineer survey work also stood a very good chance of being assigned directly to armies. Artillery batteries armed with pieces of medium weight (6in. howitzers, 60-pdr guns and 4.7in. guns), as well as units that performed simple repairs to ordnance and motor vehicles, provided rear-area security and transported supplies from railheads to divisions tended to belong to army corps.

In principle, organizations made up of non-divisional units were, like the echelons they served, both temporary in nature and variable in composition. (The practice of including the term 'army troops' in the names of various kinds of non-divisional units was in keeping with this theory.) In practice, however, there was a standard allocation of non-divisional units to army corps. As a rule, the summer of 1916 found most army corps of the Expeditionary Force with a corps troops organization consisting of corps mounted troops, two heavy artillery groups, three or four army troops companies of the Royal Engineers, two mobile ordnance workshops of the Army Ordnance Corps, one corps troops supply column and three divisional supply columns of the Army Service Corps, a corps ammunition park, a corps signal company, a wireless section, and one or more airline companies. If mining operations were taking place in the corps sector, one or more mining companies would also be assigned.

Infantry divisions

During the first year of World War I, the British Army sent six different types of infantry division to the Western Front – three types of Regular Army division, two types of Territorial Force division and one type of New Army division. In the course of the second year of the war, the number of distinct organizational schemes for Regular Army divisions was reduced to one. At the same time, the structures of Territorial Force and New Army divisions were reformed in a way that applied a single organizational scheme to all infantry divisions other than those composed primarily of units of the pre-war Regular Army.

As before, the most important organizational differences among the various types of infantry divisions serving with the Expeditionary Force in the second year of the war lay in the realm of field artillery. At first, the differences among the six field artillery establishments in use on the Western Front were the direct result of shortages. That is, the peculiar structure of Territorial Force divisions was caused by the fact that they had to be armed with obsolescent field pieces while the unique organizational scheme applied to New Army divisions was a function of a need to economize on certain kinds of artillery officers. By the start of 1916, however, these shortages had been, for the most part, remedied. After that point, the differences between the two remaining types of field artillery establishments were essentially vestigial, shadows of earlier compromises that were well on their way to being eliminated.

A second difference among the various types of infantry division concerned pioneer battalions. Before the war, the pioneer battalions of the military forces of the British Empire were exclusively associated with the Indian Army. During the first two years of the war, the institution was gradually extended to the infantry divisions of the British Army. On the Western Front, the pioneer battalions were first provided to New Army infantry divisions, then to Territorial Force infantry divisions and finally to Regular Army infantry divisions.

Apart from those related to field artillery and pioneer battalions, the changes imposed on British infantry divisions in the course of the second year of the war were applied in a uniform manner in the course of relatively short periods of time. Thus, each infantry brigade on the Western Front formed its brigade machine-gun company within the winter of 1916. Likewise, infantry divisions gained nine trench mortar batteries in the late winter and early spring of 1916. The months of May, June and July 1916 saw the transfer of all mounted troops out of infantry divisions as well as a universal restructuring of divisional trench mortar establishments.

Regular Army infantry divisions

During the first year of World War I, ten of the British infantry divisions serving on the Western Front consisted mostly of units of the pre-war Regular Army. The first six of these formations (the 1st through 6th Divisions) had belonged to the Expeditionary Force prior to the war. Because of this, they were the only fully equipped divisions to take the field until the arrival of the first New Army divisions in the summer of 1915. The other four formations (the 7th, 8th, 27th and 28th Divisions) had been cobbled together from Regular Army units that, for the most part, had been serving on garrison duty in various parts of the British Empire. Because of a shortage of artillery pieces, these latter divisions had been deployed with a reduced number of 18-pdr field guns and no 4.5in. howitzers at all.

In the course of the summer of 1915, a series of 'share the wealth' measures shifted batteries from the most favoured divisions to those that were less fortunate. At the same time, the horse artillery batteries that had been assigned to the 7th and 8th Divisions were re-armed with 18-pdrs. As a result of these efforts, the eight senior Regular Army divisions (the 1st through 8th Division) began the second year of World War I with identical field artillery establishments. That is to say, each division was provided with eight six-piece field gun batteries and two six-piece howitzer batteries. Similar efforts provided the two junior Regular Army divisions (the 27th and 28th Divisions) with field artillery establishments that were identical to those of standard New Army divisions, with 12 four-piece field gun batteries and three four-piece howitzer batteries.

The 27th and 28th Divisions were transferred to Salonika in the autumn of 1915. Their departure left all eight of the Regular Army infantry divisions with identical establishments. In addition to the retention of six-piece field

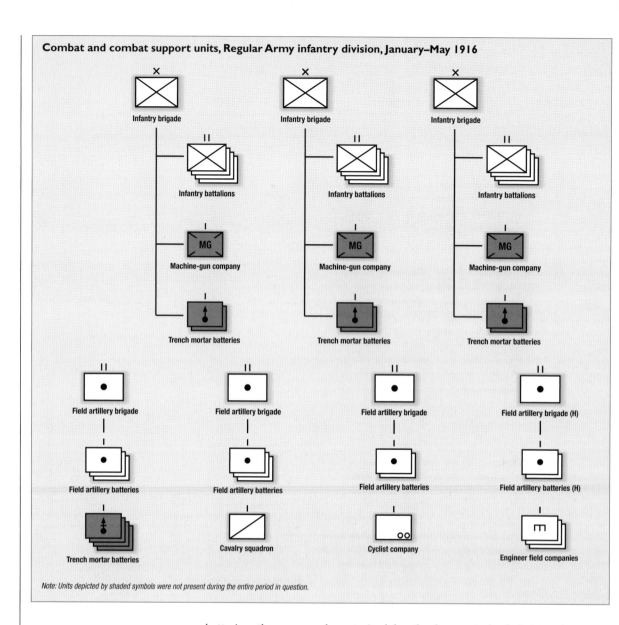

Combat and combat support units, Regular Army infantry division, January–May 1916

Infantry brigade

Infantry brigade

Infantry brigade

Infantry battalions

Infantry battalions

Infantry battalions

Machine-gun company

Machine-gun company

Machine-gun company

Trench mortar batteries

Trench mortar batteries

Trench mortar batteries

Field artillery brigade

Field artillery brigade

Field artillery brigade

Field artillery brigade (H)

Field artillery batteries

Field artillery batteries

Field artillery batteries

Field artillery batteries (H)

Trench mortar batteries

Cavalry squadron

Cyclist company

Engineer field companies

Note: Units depicted by shaded symbols were not present during the entire period in question.

batteries, these were characterized by the late arrival of divisional pioneer battalions. While New Army divisions began to get pioneer battalions in December of 1914 and Territorial Force divisions on the Western Front started to receive such units in August of 1915, the Regular Army divisions serving with the Expeditionary Force were not provided with pioneer battalions until May or June 1916.

In the late spring of 1916, the eight Regular Army divisions serving in France or Flanders underwent the same sort of changes as the other infantry divisions of the Expeditionary Force. That is to say, the mounted troops came under the direct jurisdiction of the corps headquarters, the organization of trench mortar batteries was rationalized, machine-gun companies were formed in the infantry brigades, and the howitzer batteries were parcelled out to the field gun brigades. As Regular Army divisions had three field gun brigades but only two howitzer batteries, this distribution was preceded by the recasting of the two six-piece howitzer batteries into three four-piece howitzer batteries. Moreover, as the Regular Army divisions lacked the surplus field gun batteries that other divisions transferred to the former howitzer brigades, those units were disbanded.

Combat and combat support units, Regular Army infantry division, June–December 1916

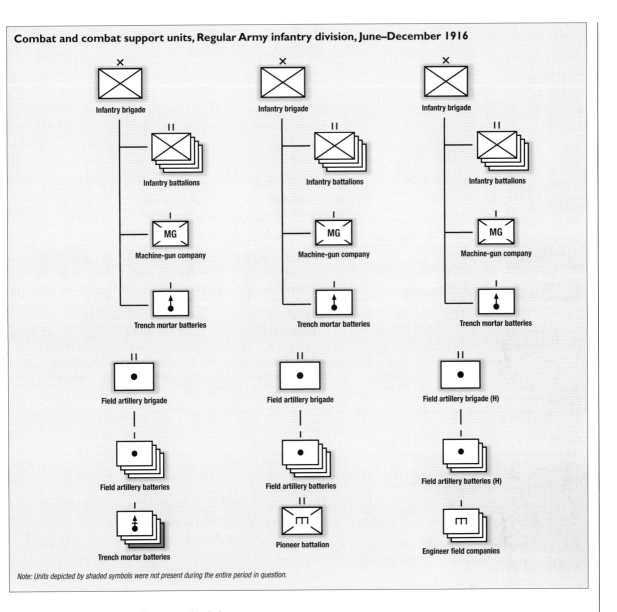

Note: Units depicted by shaded symbols were not present during the entire period in question.

Territorial Force infantry divisions

During the second year of World War I, the big organizational change for Territorial Force infantry divisions was the series of steps that were taken to increase the strength of their divisional artillery establishments. The first of these steps was a programme to replace the obsolete field artillery pieces with which Territorial Force infantry divisions had been mobilized. Between July and November 1915, the six Territorial Force infantry divisions then serving with the Expeditionary Force turned in their old 15-pdr BLC ('breech-loading converted') guns for brand-new 18-pdr field guns. In December of 1915 and January of 1916, these same divisions gave up their old 5in. howitzers in favour of new 4.5in. howitzers. As the exchange of weapons was on a 'one-for-one' basis, the Territorial Force infantry divisions retained their traditional four-piece organization for both field gun and howitzer batteries.

In January and February 1916, each of the eight Territorial Force infantry divisions then serving with the Expeditionary Force received an additional four-piece howitzer battery (these were, for the most part, provided by New Army divisions). This increased the number of field artillery batteries in each

Table 5: Re-arming the field artillery of Territorial Force divisions on the Western Front

	Arrived Western Front	Received 18-pdrs	Received 4.5in. howitzers
46th Division	March 1915	November 1915	December 1915
47th Division	March 1915	November 1915	January 1916
48th Division	March 1915	July 1915	January 1916
49th Division	April 1915	October 1915	January 1916
50th Division	April 1915	November 1915	January 1916
51st Division	May 1915	August 1915	January 1916

Combat and combat support units, Territorial Force infantry division, January–May 1916

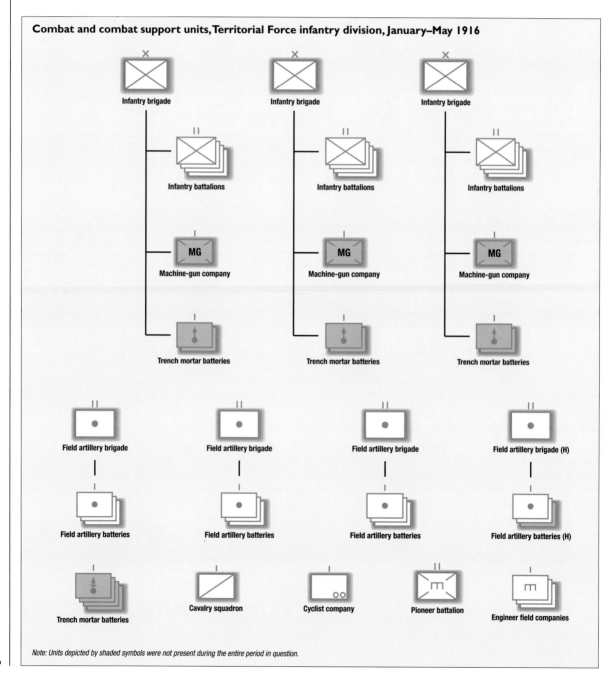

Note: Units depicted by shaded symbols were not present during the entire period in question.

Territorial Force division from 11 to 12. In April, May and June 1916, each of the Territorial Force field gun brigades in France received a fourth four-piece field gun battery (some of these were existing batteries that had been serving with other divisions; others were formed by the Territorial Force divisions themselves). This raised the number of field artillery batteries in each Territorial Force infantry division from 12 to 15.

The spring of 1915 also saw the replacement of 'thoroughbred' field artillery brigades with mixed ones. That is to say, the howitzer brigade in each Territorial Force division gave one of its three batteries to each of the field gun brigades. In return, it received one field gun battery from each of those brigades. This measure left the former field gun brigades with four batteries – three field gun batteries and a howitzer battery. Ironically, it also left the former howitzer brigade of each Territorial Force division with three field gun batteries and no howitzers at all.

In the late autumn of 1916, the former howitzer brigades were disbanded and their component batteries transferred to the three mixed brigades remaining in each division. Once assigned to their new brigades, the recently transferred field gun batteries were broken up into two-piece sections. These sections, in turn, were used to transform existing four-piece field gun batteries into six-piece field gun batteries (the three additional two-piece sections needed to complete this conversion were provided by sources other than the division itself).

The six Territorial Force infantry divisions that arrived on the Western Front in the spring of 1915 (the 46th through 51st Divisions) received their pioneer battalions in August and September of that year. These battalions were Territorial Force infantry battalions that, for the most part, had previously been attached (as the fifth or sixth battalions of infantry brigades) to Regular Army infantry divisions. The two Territorial Force infantry divisions that were re-assembled in France in the winter of 1916 (the 55th and 56th Divisions) received their pioneer battalions in the course of their reconstitution. These pioneer battalions were also Territorial Force battalions that had previously been assigned to Regular Army formations.

New Army infantry divisions

At the start of 1916, the chief organizational difference between New Army infantry divisions and Territorial Force infantry divisions was the number of field artillery batteries assigned. Where New Army infantry divisions had 16 four-piece field batteries, Territorial Force divisions had 11.

During the winter of 1916, this gap was slightly reduced by the practice of transferring a howitzer battery from a selected New Army division to each of the Territorial Force divisions. (As there were more New Army divisions on the Western Front than Territorial Force divisions, not all New Army divisions lost a howitzer battery to this scheme.) A few months later, the field artillery establishments of Territorial Force divisions and New Army divisions on the Western Front were made uniform by a programme of forming three additional field gun batteries for each Territorial Force division.

In the late spring of 1916, New Army infantry divisions reorganized their field artillery brigades in the same manner as Territorial Force divisions. That is to say, the howitzer batteries were parcelled out to the field gun brigades and the howitzer brigade formed into a howitzer-less brigade of three field gun batteries. In the late summer of 1916, New Army infantry divisions began to convert their four-piece batteries into six-piece batteries. As was also the case with the contemporary restructuring of Territorial Force divisions, this involved both the dissolution of the three-battery field gun brigade in each division and the addition of six two-piece sections.

The structural characteristics of New Army divisions were applied to two divisions that were not usually classified as such. The first of these divisions to be formed was the Guards Division. It was created in August 1915 by

Combat and combat support units, New Army infantry divisions, January–May 1916

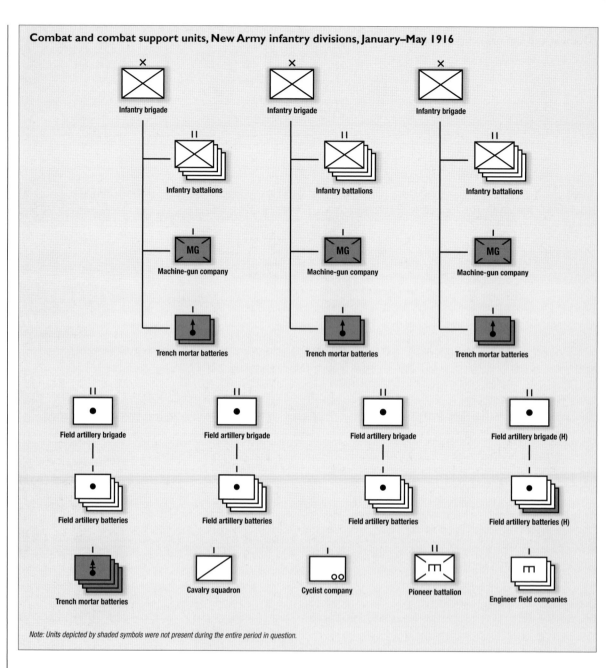

Note: Units depicted by shaded symbols were not present during the entire period in question.

combining infantry battalions formed by the five regiments of Foot Guards with the divisional artillery of the 16th (Irish) Division. The remainder of the 16th Division was later provided with a new divisional artillery establishment and joined the Expeditionary Force as a complete formation in February of 1916. The second of these divisions was the Royal Naval Division, which had been formed from surplus naval personnel at the start of the war. After serving in the defence of Antwerp (in 1914), in the Gallipoli campaign (in 1915) and on garrison duty in the Aegean (in 1916), the Royal Naval Division arrived in France in May 1916. Soon thereafter, it was provided with all of the elements needed to bring it up to the standard of a contemporary New Army division. These included a complete divisional artillery (created by the recasting of five Territorial Force field artillery brigades), seven trench mortar batteries and a pioneer battalion.

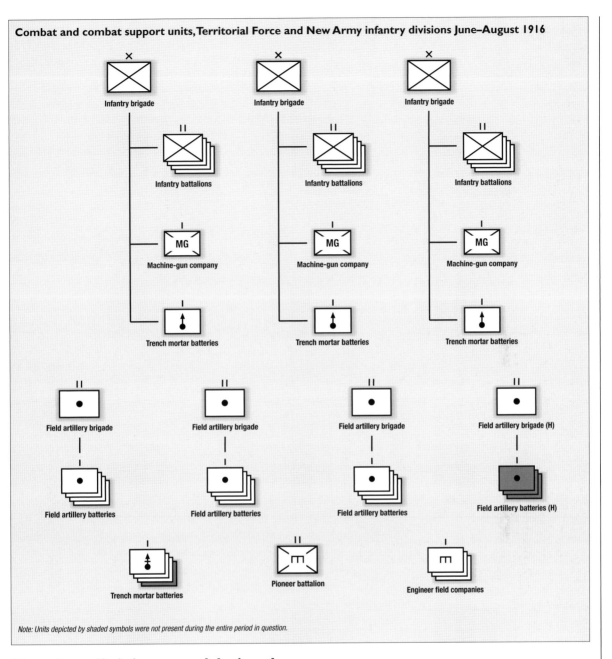

Combat and combat support units, Territorial Force and New Army infantry divisions June–August 1916

Infantry brigade

Infantry brigade

Infantry brigade

Infantry battalions

Infantry battalions

Infantry battalions

MG
Machine-gun company

MG
Machine-gun company

MG
Machine-gun company

Trench mortar batteries

Trench mortar batteries

Trench mortar batteries

Field artillery brigade

Field artillery brigade

Field artillery brigade

Field artillery brigade (H)

Field artillery batteries

Field artillery batteries

Field artillery batteries

Field artillery batteries (H)

Trench mortar batteries

Pioneer battalion

Engineer field companies

Note: Units depicted by shaded symbols were not present during the entire period in question.

Cavalry divisions and brigades

Five cavalry divisions – three from the British Army and two from the Indian Army – served with the Expeditionary Force in 1916. These were, for the most part, triangular organizations. Each of the British cavalry divisions was made up of three cavalry brigades, with each cavalry brigade consisting of three cavalry regiments and each cavalry regiment of three cavalry squadrons. Each of the Indian cavalry divisions were likewise made up of three cavalry brigades, each of which was divided into three regiments. The regiments of the Indian cavalry divisions, however, were square organizations. That is, whether they were British cavalry regiments on loan to the government of India or units formed by the Indian Army, each of these regiments preserved the four-squadron structure of the days before the creation of the Expeditionary Force. (In each of the cavalry brigades of an Indian cavalry division, one of the cavalry regiments was British and two were Indian.)

Table 6: Machine-gun section of a brigade machine-gun squadron, March 1916		
Function	**Rank in British section**	**Rank in Indian section**
Section commander	Subaltern	Subaltern*
Senior NCO	Sergeant	Dafadar
Blacksmith	Shoeing Smith	Nalbund
Junior NCO	Corporal	Lance Dafadar
Gun number	Private	Sowar
Horse holder	Private	Sowar
Driver	Driver	Driver
Cook	Cook	Cook
Bâtman (groom)	Private	Orderly
Bâtman (servant)	Private	Private*

*In an Indian machine-gun section, the section commander and his servant were British. All other men were Indian.

In addition to their cavalry regiments, cavalry brigades possessed a battery of Royal Horse Artillery and a brigade machine-gun squadron. Armed with six 13-pdr field guns, the horse artillery batteries had been a feature of cavalry brigades since September 1914. The brigade machine-gun squadrons were of more recent vintage. They were formed in February 1916 by bringing together the three regimental machine-gun sections in each brigade. As each of these regimental sections had four Vickers heavy machine guns, the brigade machine-gun squadrons that resulted from their amalgamation ended up with 12 such weapons.

When the brigade machine-gun squadrons were created, each of the regimental machine-gun sections became a 'double-section' of the new brigade machine-gun squadron. These, in turn, were broken up into two two-gun 'sections', each of which was commanded by a lieutenant or 2nd lieutenant and consisted of two non-commissioned officers, an artificer and 28 men. In most circumstances, these sections served as the basic building block of the machine-gun squadrons. However, in cases where a cavalry regiment was given an independent mission of some sort, the two sections it had provided to the brigade machine-gun squadron would be paired off to form a double-section and temporarily returned to regimental control.

Upon formation of each brigade machine-gun squadron, the cavalrymen who joined that unit were automatically enrolled in the new Machine Gun Corps.

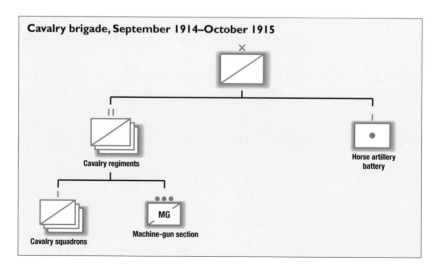

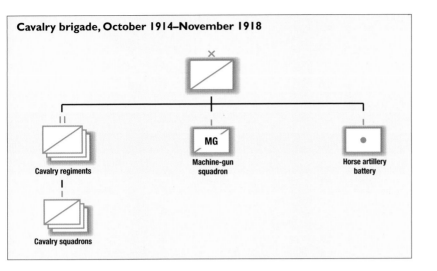

Cavalry brigade, October 1914–November 1918

Cavalry regiments

Cavalry squadrons

MG
Machine-gun squadron

Horse artillery battery

Nonetheless, the 'double-section' system ensured that these men retained a strong connection to their former regiments. In the case of the brigade machine-gun squadrons of the three British cavalry divisions, this was reflected by the custom – which continued well into 1916 – of wearing the cap badges of affiliated cavalry regiments. In the case of the brigade machine-gun squadrons of the two Indian cavalry divisions, the link between machine-gun sections and the cavalry regiments that had created them was reinforced by the practice of distinguishing 'British' machine-gun sections from 'Indian' machine gun sections. (Though the names employed to describe different jobs varied considerably, the organizational structures of both types of unit were identical.)

Dismounted cavalry units

From the very beginnings of positional warfare, elements of the five cavalry divisions serving with the Expeditionary Force had been temporarily dismounted and employed as infantry. At first, this usually took place as the

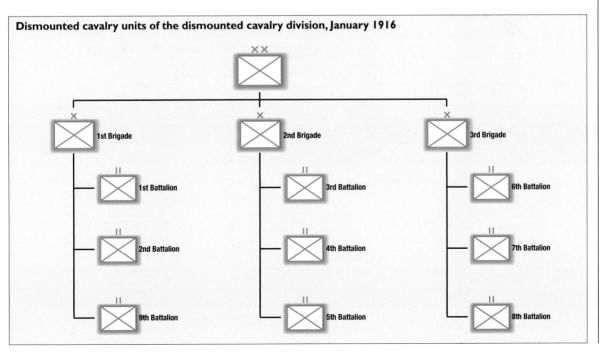

Dismounted cavalry units of the dismounted cavalry division, January 1916

1st Brigade — 1st Battalion, 2nd Battalion, 9th Battalion

2nd Brigade — 3rd Battalion, 4th Battalion, 5th Battalion

3rd Brigade — 6th Battalion, 7th Battalion, 8th Battalion

result of some sort of emergency. As a result, the dismounted cavalrymen were organized in a decidedly ad hoc fashion. By the middle of 1915, however, a pattern began to emerge. When called upon to provide men for the trenches, cavalry units and formations provided the rough equivalent of the major sub-division of their infantry counterpart. Thus, cavalry brigades formed dismounted battalions, cavalry regiments formed dismounted companies, and cavalry squadrons formed dismounted platoons.

At the end of 1915, the General Headquarters of the Expeditionary Force created the largest force of dismounted cavalry yet to be seen on the Western Front by temporarily converting a very large portion of the Cavalry Corps into the Dismounted Cavalry Division. In order to make this new formation possible, the three component divisions of the Cavalry Corps – the 1st, 2nd and 3rd Cavalry Divisions – each formed a dismounted cavalry brigade. (These brigades, quite naturally, took the numbers of the cavalry divisions that gave them birth.) The nine cavalry brigades of these three divisions, in turn, made possible the dismounted cavalry brigades by each providing a dismounted cavalry battalion. (These battalions also bore the numbers of the formations that formed them. Thus, the 6th Cavalry Brigade formed the 6th Dismounted Cavalry Battalion.) The companies and machine-gun sections needed to create the dismounted cavalry battalions were produced, at a rate of one dismounted company and one machine-gun section per cavalry regiment, by the 27 cavalry regiments of the Cavalry Corps.

The 6th Dismounted Cavalry Battalion, January 1916

- 1st Royal Dragoons
- 3rd Dragoon Guards
- North Somerset Yeomanry
- MG — 'Brigaded' machine guns

The 6th Dismounted Cavalry Battalion, January 1916

In January of 1916, each of the three regiments of the 6th Cavalry Brigade provided two elements to the 6th Dismounted Cavalry Battalion. The first of these was a dismounted cavalry company of some 320 officers and men. The second was a machine-gun section of four Vickers machine guns. Soon after these elements were brought together, the three machine-gun sections were 'brigaded' to form an ad hoc machine-gun company, which was promptly taken out of the battalion and employed as a separate unit.

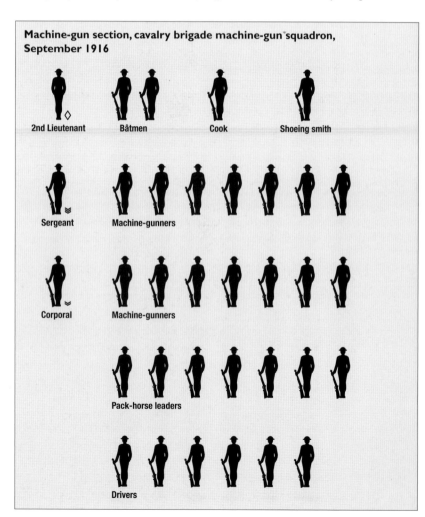

Machine-gun section, cavalry brigade machine-gun squadron, September 1916

2nd Lieutenant — Bâtmen — Cook — Shoeing smith

Sergeant — Machine-gunners

Corporal — Machine-gunners

Pack-horse leaders

Drivers

Because it was, in effect, a shadow of the organizational framework of the cavalry corps, the framework of the Dismounted Cavalry Division had a number of organizational peculiarities. It was, first of all, a triangular organization rather than a square one. That is, instead of four companies in each battalion and four infantry battalions in each brigade, it had three dismounted cavalry companies in each battalion and three dismounted cavalry battalions in each brigade. Because of this, the correspondence between dismounted cavalry units and their infantry counterparts was not always exact. In particular, while dismounted cavalry battalions were of roughly the same size as infantry battalions, dismounted cavalry companies were considerably larger than infantry companies.

Dismounted cavalry companies consisted of six numbered platoons. This 'hexagonal' organization, which mirrored that of cavalry brigade machine-gun squadrons, served two purposes. The first was to accommodate the fact that dismounted cavalry companies were much larger than their infantry counterparts. The second allowed each of the component squadrons of a cavalry regiment to form two dismounted platoons. Thus, A Squadron could form No. 1 and No. 2 Platoons, B Squadron could form No. 3 and No. 4 Platoons, and C Squadron could form No. 5 and No. 6 Platoons.

Cavalry regiments and squadrons

During the first two years of the war, the practice of assigning a squadron of cavalry to each infantry division put divisional cavalry squadrons in the uncomfortable position of getting operational instructions from the officer commanding divisional mounted troops and administrative ones from a separate regimental headquarters. In the late spring of 1916, this problem was solved by the creation of corps cavalry regiments. These initially consisted of the regimental headquarters of an existing cavalry regiment and the divisional cavalry squadrons of all assigned infantry divisions. Later, as infantry divisions moved from one army corps to another, the link between them and their formerly assigned divisional cavalry squadrons was broken. This made possible the return to the standard three-squadron organization for a war-strength cavalry regiment and the return of many squadrons to their parent regiments.

The institution of the corps cavalry regiment dealt the deathblow to the pre-war convention that only the mounted units of the Regular Army could be

Army corps	Regimental headquarters	First squadron	Second squadron	Third squadron (parent regiment)
I	1st South Irish Horse	B	C	E
II	Queen's Own Yorkshire Dragoons	A	B	C
III	Duke of Lancaster's Own	C	D	D (Surrey Yeomanry)
IV	1st King Edward's Horse	A	B	C
V	Glasgow Yeomanry	A	B	B (Lothians and Border Horse)
VI	Northamptonshire Yeomanry	A	B	C
VII	1st North Irish Horse	A	D	E
IX	Wiltshire Yeomanry	A	B	C (Hampshire Yeomanry)
X	2nd North Irish Horse	B	C	Service (6th Dragoons)
XIII	Northumberland Yeomanry	A	B	C
XV	2nd South Irish Horse	A	B	D (Royal Wiltshire Yeomanry)
XVII	Yorkshire Hussars Yeomanry	A	B	C

Table 7: Corps cavalry regiments, June 1916

	Cavalry regiment 1914	Cavalry or Yeomanry regiment 1916	Corps cavalry regiment
Table 8: Squadrons of cavalry regiments, 1914–16			
Major (CO)	1	1	1
Captain (second-in-command)	1	1	1
Subalterns	4	4	4
Sergeant-major	1	1	1
Quartermaster sergeant	1	1	1
Sergeants	8	8	8
Farrier sergeant	1	1	1
Shoeing smiths	4	4	4
Saddler	1	1	1
Trumpeters	2	2	2
Corporals	8	8	8
Signallers	3	0	0
Privates	104	104	90
Drivers	7	9	9
Bâtmen	12	12	12
Total	158	157	143

properly called 'cavalry'. In an army where most other distinctions between Regular, Territorial Force and Special Reserve units were rapidly fading away, it was simply too much trouble to maintain an artificial distinction between Regular Army 'cavalry', Territorial Force 'Yeomanry' and Special Reserve 'Horse'. Indeed, only one of the divisional cavalry squadrons serving on the Western Front during the second year of World War I was, strictly speaking a 'cavalry' unit. This was the Household Cavalry Divisional Squadron of the Guards Division, a wartime unit made up of men from the three regiments of Household Cavalry – the 1st Life Guards, the 2nd Life Guards and the Royal Horse Guards. All of the other divisional cavalry squadrons of British infantry divisions of the Expeditionary Force belonged either to Yeomanry regiments, one of the two regiments of Irish Horse, or King Edward's Horse. Likewise, nearly all of the squadrons of the corps cavalry regiments belonged to units of either the Territorial Force or the Special Reserve. (The exception that proves this rule was the 'service' squadron of the 6th Dragoons. This was a wartime unit formed from men who were surplus to the needs of the regularly constituted squadrons of that regiment.)

The fast-fading distinction between 'cavalry' and horse-soldier units of other types was recognized by the edition of *War Establishments* that was published in September of 1916. These provided for only two varieties of cavalry regiments for service with British Army formations – a corps cavalry regiment for service with army corps and a 'cavalry or Yeomanry' regiment for service within the cavalry brigades of cavalry divisions. British cavalry regiments serving with the two Indian cavalry divisions on the Western Front were organized in accordance with a separate 'special for India' edition of the *War Establishments*. The definitive feature of the organizational framework of these units was the division of each regiment into four squadrons rather than three.

The chief difference between the corps cavalry regiments and the cavalry regiments of British cavalry divisions was the number of 'sabres' assigned to each squadron. While a squadron of a corps cavalry regiment had but 90 privates (other than specialists) in its ranks, a squadron serving with a cavalry

Table 9: Headquarters of cavalry regiments, 1914–16

	Cavalry regiment 1914	Cavalry or Yeomanry regiment 1916	Corps Cavalry regiment 1916
Lieutenant-colonel (CO)	1	1	1
Major (second-in-command)	1	1	1
Adjutant	1	1	1
Signalling officer	1	1	1
Quartermaster	1	1	1
Medical officer (RAMC)	1	1	1
Veterinary officer (RAVC)	1	1	0
Regimental sergeant-major	1	1	1
Quartermaster sergeant	1	1	1 *
Transport sergeant	1	1	1
Orderly room clerk	1	1	1
Sergeant trumpeter	1	1	1
Sergeant cook	1	1	1
Signalling sergeant	1	1	0
Farrier	1	1	1
Saddler sergeant	1	1	1
Armourer (AOC)	1	1	1
Saddletree maker	1	1	1
Signallers	5	5	5
Orderlies (medical officer)	2	2	2
Orderly (commanding officer)	0	0	1
Drivers	7	10	3
Bâtmen	13	13	10
Water duties men (RAMC)	3	3	3
Total	48	51	40

*The quartermaster sergeant of a corps cavalry regiment bore the rank of a warrant officer and the title of 'regimental quartermaster sergeant'. The quartermaster sergeants of other types of cavalry regiments were non-commissioned officers.

division had 104 such men. As long the stalemate on the Western Front kept cavalry divisions from fulfilling their primary function of operational reconnaissance in mobile warfare, these extra men facilitated the formation of dismounted cavalry units. That is to say, they made it possible for each squadron to despatch two dismounted platoons for service in the trenches and still retain a sufficient number of men to maintain the capability to quickly reconstitute the squadron. (Whilst largely a matter of caring for horses, this was also a matter of practicing the skills associated with operational reconnaissance and mounted combat.)

Irrespective of the number of 'sabres', all squadrons of British cavalry, Yeomanry or Horse serving with the Expeditionary Force were divided into four troops. When the machine-gun sections of cavalry regiments were abolished in favour of the brigade machine-gun squadrons, a portion of these troops (usually two per squadron) were given 'Hotchkiss rifles'. These automatic rifles were lighter versions of the Hotchkiss machine guns that were then being employed by the French Army and the Royal Flying Corps. In September 1916, the official allowance of such weapons was set at four per squadron, which allowed every troop to possess a Hotchkiss rifle of its own.

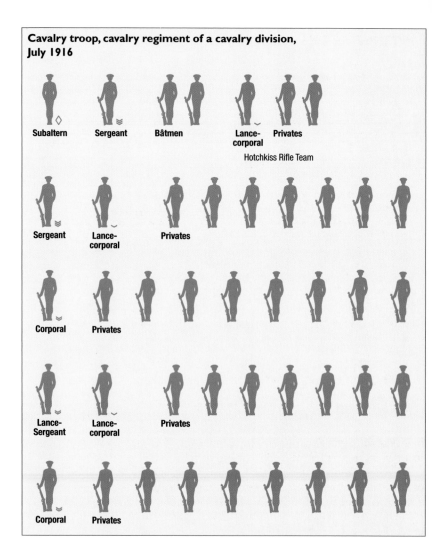

Cavalry troop, cavalry regiment of a cavalry division, July 1916

Subaltern Sergeant Bâtmen Lance-corporal Privates

Hotchkiss Rifle Team

Sergeant Lance-corporal Privates

Corporal Privates

Lance-Sergeant Lance-corporal Privates

Corporal Privates

Corps cyclist battalions and divisional cyclist companies

At the same time that divisional cavalry squadrons were transferred to the corps cavalry regiments, divisional cyclist companies were assembled into corps cyclist battalions. As these cyclist battalions had no previous existence, there was no need to return particular companies to particular battalions. Instead, the cyclist companies serving in each army corps in May or June 1916 were, in most cases, simply detached from their divisions and formed into a new unit. (In the remaining cases, cyclist companies were either assigned to the cyclist battalions of corps other than their own or broken up in order to reinforce cyclist battalions that were under strength.)

The mission of corps cyclist battalions was similar to that of the divisional cyclist companies. Divisional cyclist companies had been designed to relieve divisional cavalry squadrons of those reconnaissance and security duties that did not require the employment of skilled horsemen. These included patrols in areas that were well provided with roads, and missions that involved a great deal of dismounted work. While all British cavalrymen of World War I were trained to fight on foot as well as on horseback, the act of dismounting deprived a cavalry unit of the services of the men detailed to care for the horses. As one man could only manage four horses or so, the transition from saddle to boot cost a cavalry unit some 25 per cent of its rifle strength. A cyclist unit, however, did not have to worry about its mounts running off on their

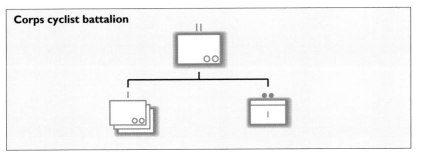

Corps cyclist battalion

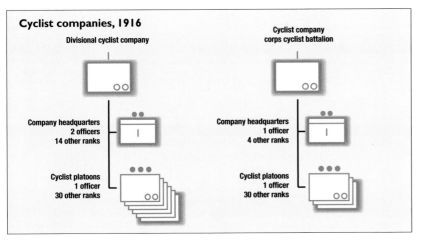

Cyclist companies, 1916

Divisional cyclist company

Company headquarters
2 officers
14 other ranks

Cyclist platoons
1 officer
30 other ranks

Cyclist company
corps cyclist battalion

Company headquarters
1 officer
4 other ranks

Cyclist platoons
1 officer
30 other ranks

own accord or being hit by stray small-arms fire. It could thus put every one of its rifles into the firing line.

Cyclist battalions were relatively small units, with an authorized strength of some 322 officers and men. (A contemporary infantry battalion had an authorized strength of 999 officers and men.) The three companies of each cyclist battalion were, at 98 officers and men, likewise much smaller than either British infantry companies of the day (229 officers and men) or the standard divisional cyclist companies of the first two years of the war (204 officers and men). Because of this, the formation of corps cyclist battalions created a surplus of unassigned men. A few of these found jobs in the headquarters of the new corps cyclist battalions. Most, however, were sent to other units, with a considerable number ending up in military police units and trench mortar batteries.

The standard building block of both divisional cyclist companies and the cyclist companies of corps cyclist battalions was the 31-man cyclist platoon. (A divisional cyclist company had six such platoons. A cyclist company of a corps cyclist battalion had three.) Each of these platoons consisted of a small headquarters and four sections. The headquarters was made up of the platoon commander (a lieutenant or second lieutenant), a sergeant and a bâtman. Each section consisted of a section leader (who usually ranked as either a corporal or a lance-corporal) and six men.

As long as the Expeditionary Force was locked in positional warfare, most of the reconnaissance and security work carried out on the ground was performed by patrols provided by infantry battalions. As a result, cyclist units spent the middle years of the war in much the same way as their comrades in the divisional cavalry squadrons and the corps cavalry regiments. They trained for the resumption of mobile warfare; patrolled the roads, woods and fields behind the front lines; escorted prisoners of war; and provided working parties for various fatigues and engineering projects.

Mounted troops

Between August 1914 and the late spring of 1916, the commanders of the cavalry squadron and cyclist company in each infantry division answered directly to the 'officer commanding, divisional mounted troops'. When the divisional cavalry squadrons were assembled into corps cavalry regiments and the divisional cyclist companies were formed into corps cyclist battalions, the 'divisional mounted troops' in each infantry division were disbanded. At the same time, a similar organization, known as 'corps mounted troops', was formed for each army corps. In addition to serving as the organizational home for the corps cavalry regiment and cyclist battalion, the corps mounted troops provided a berth for the motor machine-gun battery that was provided to many army corps in the middle of 1916.

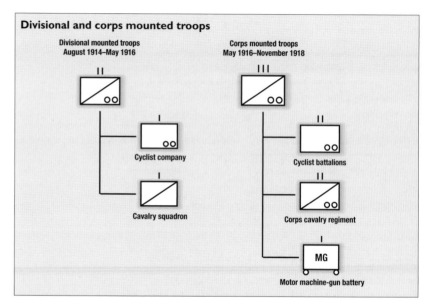

Infantry brigades and battalions

At the start of World War I, the infantry brigades of the Expeditionary Force were the most perfectly 'square' combat organizations ever fielded by a 20th-century army. That is to say, each brigade consisted of four battalions, each battalion consisted of four companies, each company consisted of four platoons and each platoon consisted of four sections. The one organizational feature that marred the perfect symmetry of this arrangement was the presence of a two-gun machine-gun section in each infantry battalion.

During the first year of the war, the basic structure of the infantry brigade of the Expeditionary Force remained unchanged. Indeed, as new infantry brigades joined the Expeditionary Force, they often cast off their old organizational frameworks in order to adopt that of the Regular Army infantry brigades of the original Expeditionary Force. (The infantry brigades to do this were those of six Territorial Force divisions and one Canadian division that reported for duty on the Western Front in the winter and spring of 1915.) By October 1915, however, it was clear that the simple 'four-by-four' structure was not going to be able to accommodate the large number of machine guns that would soon be provided to each infantry brigade. The old structure could handle the issue of eight extra machine guns to each infantry brigade of the Expeditionary Force that took place in the spring of 1915. It could not, however, manage the three-fold increase in the number of machine guns authorized to each infantry brigade that occurred in October of that year. That is, a battalion machine-gun section could easily absorb two additional machine guns by the simple

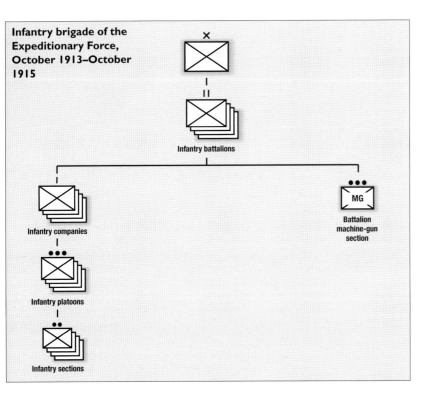

Infantry brigade of the Expeditionary Force, October 1913–October 1915

Infantry battalions

Infantry companies

Infantry platoons

Infantry sections

MG — Battalion machine-gun section

expedient of adding a few more men and forming two extra machine-gun crews. This platoon-sized unit, however, could not provide crews for four additional heavy machine guns and eight of the new Lewis light machine guns.

The War Office solved the problem of finding proper organizational homes for the machine guns by dividing the responsibility for these weapons between two different echelons. The heavy machine guns that had previously been the exclusive concern of battalion machine-gun sections would become the

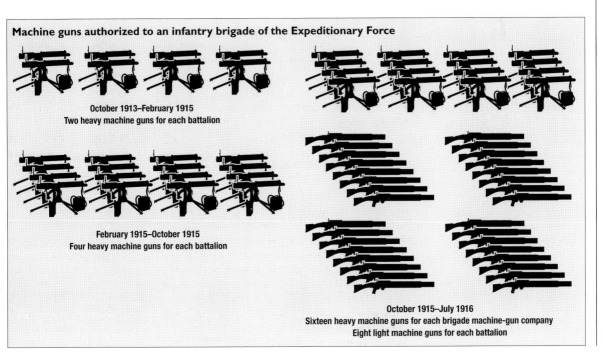

Machine guns authorized to an infantry brigade of the Expeditionary Force

October 1913–February 1915
Two heavy machine guns for each battalion

February 1915–October 1915
Four heavy machine guns for each battalion

October 1915–July 1916
Sixteen heavy machine guns for each brigade machine-gun company
Eight light machine guns for each battalion

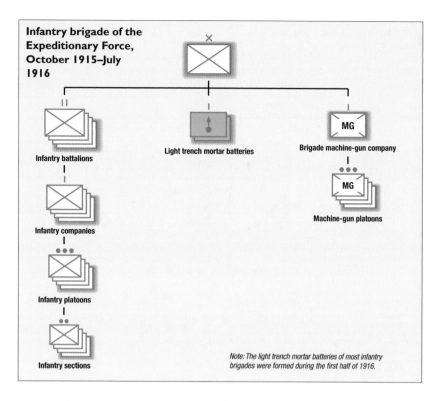

Infantry brigade of the Expeditionary Force, October 1915–July 1916

Infantry battalions

Infantry companies

Infantry platoons

Infantry sections

Light trench mortar batteries

Brigade machine-gun company

Machine-gun platoons

Note: The light trench mortar batteries of most infantry brigades were formed during the first half of 1916.

domain of units of an entirely new type, brigade machine-gun companies. Each of these would be created by bringing together all of the battalion machine-gun sections of a given brigade. As there were such sections in each brigade, the resulting company would have four component platoons, each of which would be armed with four heavy machine guns. The Lewis light machine guns would be given, at a rate of eight guns per battalion, to infantry battalions. As these battalions had just lost their machine-gun sections, this meant that the Lewis guns would be given, at a rate of two per company, to the component infantry companies of those battalions.

On the eve of the battle of the Somme (which began on 1 July 1916), the official allotment of Lewis guns for a battalion of infantry was doubled. This meant that there would be a sufficient number of Lewis guns to provide one such weapon to each of the four platoons of an infantry company. Just as it took several months for the increased allowances for machine guns laid down in February and October of 1915 to be applied to all infantry brigades on the Western Front, it took quite a bit of time for all infantry battalions fighting on the Western Front to receive this extra ration of portable firepower.

Pioneer battalions

A pioneer battalion was a hybrid unit that was expected to be able to fulfil all of the tasks normally associated with an infantry battalion and many of those otherwise performed by the field companies of the Royal Engineers. Because of the first mission, a pioneer battalion of 1916 was organized in exactly the same manner as a contemporary infantry battalion. Because of the second, it was provided with a healthy allowance of engineer stores – tools, explosives and building materials, as well as the wagons, horses and drivers needed to carry them.

A few pioneer units had been raised as such. That is to say, the men who joined these units upon (or soon after) their formation were fully aware that they were joining a pioneer unit and not a unit of any other sort. Most of the pioneer units that served with the Expeditionary Force in 1916, however, had originally been formed (or, in the case of many pre-war Territorial Force units,

Table 10: Pioneer battalions of the Expeditionary Force, 1 July 1916

Division	Date Assigned	Contingent	Battalion	Regiment
Guards	August 1915	Regular Army (wartime)	4th	Coldstream Guards
1st	May 1916	Territorial Force	1/6th	Welsh Regiment
2nd	June 1916	New Army	10th	Duke of Cornwall's Light Infantry
3rd	May 1916	New Army	20th	King's Royal Rifle Corps
4th	June 1916	New Army	21st	West Yorkshire Regiment
5th	June 1916	Territorial Force	6th	Argyll and Sutherland Highlanders
6th	April 1916	New Army	11th	Leicestershire Regiment
7th	May 1916	New Army	24th	Manchester Regiment
8th	July 1916	New Army	22nd	Durham Light Infantry
9th	February 1915	New Army	9th	Seaforth Highlanders
11th	December 1914	New Army	6th	East Yorkshire
12th	January 1915	New Army	9th	North Staffordshire Regiment
14th	January 1915	New Army	11th	The King's (Liverpool Regiment)
15th	January 1915	New Army	9th	Gordon Highlanders
16th	December 1914	New Army	11th	Hampshire Regiment
17th	March 1915	New Army	7th	York and Lancaster
18th	May 1915	New Army	8th	Royal Sussex
19th	June 1916	New Army	5th	South Wales Borderers
20th	July 1915	New Army	11th	Durham Light Infantry
21st	January 1915	New Army	14th	Northumberland Fusiliers
23rd	January 1915	New Army	9th	South Staffordshire Regiment
24th	April 1915	New Army	12th	Sherwood Foresters
29th	May 1916	Territorial Force	1/2nd	Monmouthshire Regiment
30th	May 1915	New Army	11th	South Lancashire Regiment
31st	May 1915	New Army	12th	King's Own Yorkshire Light Infantry
32nd	June 1915	New Army	17th	Northumberland Fusiliers
33rd	July 1915	New Army	18th	Middlesex Regiment
34th	August 1915	New Army	18th	Northumberland Fusiliers
35th	August 1915	New Army	19th	Northumberland Fusiliers
36th	January 1915	New Army	16th	Royal Irish Rifles
37th	April 1915	New Army	9th	North Staffordshire Regiment
38th	February 1915	New Army	19th	Welsh Regiment
39th	July 1915	New Army	13th	Gloucestershire Regiment
40th	September 1915	New Army	12th	Yorkshire Regiment
41st	October 1915	New Army	19th	Middlesex Regiment
46th	September 1915	Territorial Force	1/1st	Monmouthshire Regiment
47th	September 1915	Territorial Force	1/4th	Royal Welch Fusiliers
48th	August 1915	Territorial Force	1/5th	Royal Sussex
49th	September 1915	Territorial Force	1/3rd	Monmouthshire Regiment
50th	November 1915	Territorial Force	1/7th	Durham Light Infantry
51st	August 1915	Territorial Force	1/8th	Royal Scots
55th	January 1916	Territorial Force	1/4th	South Lancashire
56th	Feb 1916	Territorial Force	1/5th	Cheshire Regiment
60th	June 1916	Territorial Force	1/12th	Loyal North Lancashire
61st	May 1916	Territorial Force	1/5th	Duke of Cornwall's Light Infantry
63rd	June 1916	New Army	14th	Worcestershire Regiment

mobilized) as ordinary infantry battalions and subsequently converted. In either case, the men who filled the ranks of pioneer battalions were supposed to be men who were already accustomed to heavy labour. More specifically, they were supposed to be miners, construction labourers, metal workers or practitioners of various building trades. Unfortunately, the demand for pioneer battalions was much greater than the supply of battalions composed mostly of this sort of men. As a result, many soldiers did not become acquainted with the engineering side of a pioneer's duties until after they had joined a pioneer battalion.

Whether or not they had spent any time as ordinary infantry units, all pioneer battalions were formally affiliated with an infantry regiment. They were, moreover, officially listed as component battalions of that infantry regiment. Thus, the battalion that was informally known as the Glamorgan Pioneers was, strictly speaking, the 19th Battalion (Pioneers), The Welsh Regiment. In keeping with this practice, the one Regular Army unit that was raised as a pioneer battalion, the Guards Pioneer Battalion of the Guards Division, was quickly renamed the 4th Battalion (Pioneers), Coldstream Guards. Possession of an informal name that contained the word 'pioneers' was a sure sign that a particular pioneer battalion had either been initially raised as a pioneer battalion or converted into a pioneer unit soon after its creation. Thus, the Severn Valley Pioneers, the St Helen's Pioneers and the Teesside Pioneers were all raised as pioneer units, while the 1st Tyneside Pioneers and the North Eastern Railway Pioneers were both converted into pioneer units within five months of being formed.

Artillery brigades and groups

At the start of the 20th century, the most important echelon of command within the Royal Regiment of Artillery was the battery. The battery was not only the basic tactical unit, but also the focus of most administration and the chief repository of tradition. Between 1901 and 1915, however, the battery began to lose many of its functions to the 'brigade', a lieutenant-colonel's command that was slowly evolving from a task force of two or more otherwise independent batteries to a permanently constituted unit in its own right. In the course of the first year of the war, two organizational reforms made the artillery brigade more important than it ever had been. The first of these was the restructuring of the field artillery establishments of New Army divisions, which reduced the rank of most battery commanders from major to captain and deprived batteries of their

Table 11: Artillery batteries of the British Army present for duty on 5 August of each year			
	1914	1915	1916
Siege batteries	6	55	221
Field batteries	304	1,024	936
Heavy batteries	26	93	127
Horse artillery batteries	40	49	44
Mountain batteries	12	12	12

Table 12: Artillery batteries of the Expeditionary Force present for duty on 5 August of each year			
	1914	1915	1916
Siege batteries	0	26	132
Field batteries	72	312	546
Heavy batteries	6	32	62
Horse artillery batteries	5	18	21
Mountain batteries	0	2	0

Table 13: Allocation of siege artillery pieces to the Expeditionary Force						
	15in. howitzer	12in. howitzer	9.2in. howitzer	8in. howitzer	6in. howitzer	6in. gun
1 October 1914	0	0	0	0	24	0
1 January 1915	0	0	1	0	24	8
1 April 1915	1	0	8	0	32	8
1 July 1915	3	0	14	8	48	8
1 October 1915	3	1	20	24	72	24
1 January 1916	5	6	24	32	76	24
1 April 1916	6	20	44	58	92	32
1 July 1916	8	30	88	64	192	32
1 October 1916	10	32	140	100	312	32
1 January 1917	10	28	176	120	424	48

unique numbers. (The batteries of these divisions had names that were formed by combining the number of their parent brigade with a letter of the alphabet. Thus, the senior battery of the 104th Brigade, Royal Field Artillery became A/104 Battery, Royal Field Artillery.) The second of the 'brigade bolstering reforms' was the creation of a large number of 'brigades, Royal Garrison Artillery'. These served as the organizational homes for the heavy batteries that were withdrawn from infantry divisions in the winter of 1915, as well as the many siege and heavy batteries that were then being formed as non-divisional units.

In the course of 1916, a series of reforms to the artillery establishments of infantry divisions solidified the position of the brigade as the basic tactical and administrative unit of the Royal Field Artillery. At the same time, 'brigades, Royal Garrison Artillery' were moving in the opposite direction, changing their internal orders of battle with such frequency that they had become, in effect, free-floating headquarters. In the spring of 1916, this change was institutionalized by an order that transformed all 'brigades, Royal Garrison Artillery' then serving with the Expeditionary Force into 'heavy artillery groups'.

Field artillery brigades

A field artillery brigade of late 1915 or early 1916 could have had eight, 12, 16 or 18 field pieces assigned to it. These field pieces could have been organized into two, three or four batteries. The eight-piece, two-battery field artillery brigades might have been equipped with either 5in. or 4.5in howitzers. The 12-piece field artillery brigades might have been divided into two six-piece batteries or three four-piece batteries. In the former case, the weapons could have been either 18-pdr field guns or 4.5in. howitzers. In the latter case, the weapons could have been either 18-pdr field guns or 15-pdr BLC field guns. The 16-piece field artillery brigades invariably consisted of four four-piece batteries and were invariably armed with 18-pdrs. Though always divided into three six-piece batteries, 18-piece field artillery brigades were equipped with either 18-pdr field guns or 4.5in. howitzers. In short, the start of 1916 found the Expeditionary Force with nine distinct ways of organizing a brigade of field artillery.

The first step towards eliminating this organizational cacophony was the re-arming of the field batteries of Territorial Force divisions. This effort, which began in July 1915 and was completed by the end of January 1916, replaced each obsolete field piece serving on the Western Front with its up-to-date counterpart. Between July and November 1915, Territorial Force field gun batteries exchanged their old 15-pdr BLC field guns for new 18-pdr field guns. In December 1915 and January 1916, Territorial Force howitzer batteries swapped their old 5in. howitzers for new 4.5in. howitzers.

The second step in the restructuring of the field artillery of the Expeditionary Force was the provision of additional howitzer batteries to those divisions that had fewer than three such units. This 'share the wealth' scheme took complete four-piece howitzer batteries out of New Army divisions that had four such units and gave them to divisions that had only one or two. The first beneficiary of this programme was the 28th Infantry Division, which received two four-piece howitzer batteries in August of 1915. (This gave that formation a total of three four-piece howitzer batteries.) The vast majority of these transfers, however, took place in February 1916, when eight four-piece howitzer batteries were taken out of New Army divisions and parcelled out to the eight Territorial Force divisions then serving on the Western Front. (This reform had the effect of giving each infantry division in the Expeditionary Force a minimum of 12 4.5in howitzers and so retiring the previously common two-battery, eight-piece organizational scheme for howitzer-armed field artillery brigades.)

The assignment of an additional howitzer battery to each Territorial Force howitzer brigade was followed, in May 1915, by the assignment of an additional field gun battery to each Territorial Force field gun brigade. As the latter brigades already consisted of three batteries, the extra battery formed the fourth battery of each brigade. As all of the batteries involved in this transfer were four-piece batteries, it had the effect of increasing the number of field guns in each Territorial Force field gun brigade from 12 to 16.

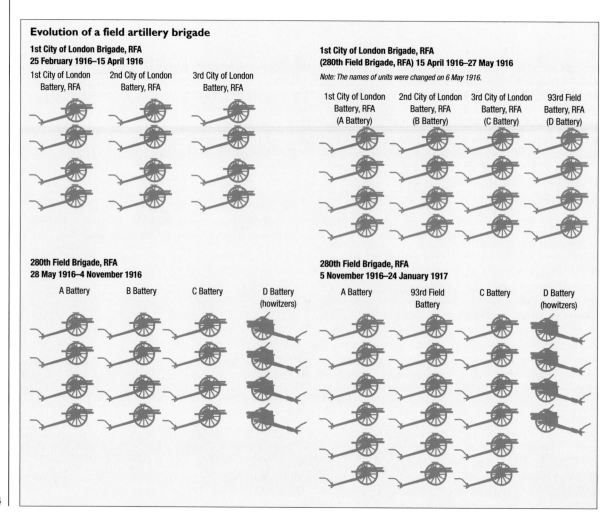

Evolution of a field artillery brigade

1st City of London Brigade, RFA
25 February 1916–15 April 1916

1st City of London Battery, RFA

2nd City of London Battery, RFA

3rd City of London Battery, RFA

1st City of London Brigade, RFA
(280th Field Brigade, RFA) 15 April 1916–27 May 1916

Note: The names of units were changed on 6 May 1916.

1st City of London Battery, RFA (A Battery)

2nd City of London Battery, RFA (B Battery)

3rd City of London Battery, RFA (C Battery)

93rd Field Battery, RFA (D Battery)

280th Field Brigade, RFA
28 May 1916–4 November 1916

A Battery

B Battery

C Battery

D Battery (howitzers)

280th Field Brigade, RFA
5 November 1916–24 January 1917

A Battery

93rd Field Battery

C Battery

D Battery (howitzers)

When combined with the re-allocation of howitzer batteries that had preceded it, this reform also had the effect of equalizing the artillery strength of infantry divisions. That is, the middle of 1916 found nearly all the British infantry divisions on the Western Front with 48 18-pdr field guns and 12 4.5in. howitzers. (The only divisions that departed from this norm were the handful of New Army divisions that had yet to lose their fourth howitzer battery.)

The three 'equalizing' reforms of late 1915 and early 1916 were followed, in May and June 1916, by a reshuffling of batteries that touched every single field artillery brigade then serving on the Western Front. Whereas the previous reforms had been aimed at reducing the differences between the field artillery establishments of infantry divisions, the reshuffling was based on the way that field artillery was actually being employed. In the course of the second year of the war, many divisional artillery commanders had adopted the practice of forming mixed groups of field gun and howitzer batteries. While these did a better job of covering an assigned sector than traditional 'thoroughbred' brigades, the forming of mixed brigades put divisional field artillery establishments in the awkward position of having one organizational structure for administration and another one for tactical employment.

To remedy this problem, the Expeditionary Force adopted a scheme for replacing uniformly armed field artillery brigades with brigades that contained both field guns and howitzers. In New Army and Territorial Force divisions (which now had very similar field artillery establishments) the creation of mixed brigades was largely a matter of reshuffling existing batteries. (As there were only three howitzer batteries in each New Army or Territorial Force division, the result of this game of military musical chairs was that one of the four field artillery brigades in each such division did not get a howitzer battery and thus remained a 'thoroughbred' unit.) In the eight Regular divisions still on the Western Front, more radical surgery was required. The howitzer brigade in each division was dissolved and its two component batteries were each deprived of one two-piece section. These sections were joined together to form a new battery, thereby giving each Regular division three four-piece howitzer batteries. Each of these batteries was then attached to one of the remaining brigades.

Between October 1916 and January 1917, a final set of reforms eliminated all of the remaining structural differences among the field artillery brigades of the Expeditionary Force. The fourth brigades of Territorial Force and New Army divisions – the only field artillery brigades that were still armed exclusively with field guns – were disbanded. At the same time, the remaining four-piece batteries of the Expeditionary Force were provided with a third two-piece section and thus converted into six-piece batteries. Thus, by 1 February 1917, the field artillery establishments of all British infantry divisions of the Expeditionary Force – whether Regular Army, Territorial Force or New Army – consisted of three uniformly organized field artillery brigades, each of three six-piece field gun batteries and one six-piece howitzer battery.

As the number of artillery brigades of various types increased, the old custom of designating them with Roman numerals began to fall by the wayside. One reason for this was the fact that, with the possible exception of masons who specialized in the making of cornerstones, few Britons of the early 20th century were ever required to deal with Roman numerals larger than the 'XII' found on many public clocks of the day. Another was the problem that Roman numerals created for those poor souls who, when reading a mimeographed or hand-written order by the light of a flickering candle, had to quickly differentiate 'CCIX' from 'CLIV'. (As the numbers designating army corps were relatively low ones and documents listing multiple army corps were more likely to be read in reasonably civilized surroundings, the custom of using Roman numerals to distinguish such formations was retained throughout the war.)

The 4.7in. gun, which had equipped the majority of heavy batteries sent to the Western Front during the first year of World War I, was still a common sight in 1916. By the middle of 1917, however, this obsolescent weapon had been entirely replaced by the 60-pdr. (Library of Congress)

Heavy and siege brigades

Prior to World War I, the heavy and siege batteries of the Royal Garrison Artillery were sometimes formed into heavy and siege brigades. Like field artillery brigades, these units had both a tactical function (directing the fire of assigned batteries) and an administrative one (linking assigned batteries to higher echelons of command). To those ends, heavy and siege brigades had headquarters that were very much like those of field artillery brigades. Unlike field artillery brigades, however, siege and heavy brigades did not get intimately involved in the supply of ammunition to their component batteries. This was due to the fact that, rather than depending upon a brigade-level ammunition column, each siege or heavy battery of the British Army possessed a small ammunition column of its own.

Because siege and heavy batteries possessed a high degree of logistical self-reliance, it was possible to deploy them as independent units. Indeed, one of the first casualties of the mobilization of the six heavy batteries of the original Expeditionary Force was the dissolution of the two heavy brigades that had provided them with an organizational home during the long years of peace. The two brigade headquarters of the Royal Garrison Artillery that were mobilized in August 1914, moreover, belonged to units that were not included in the original Expeditionary Force. (These were the two siege brigades that were created by the expansion of the three peacetime siege companies of the Royal Garrison Artillery. According to the mobilization plans executed at the start of the war, these were only to be deployed in the event that the Expeditionary Force found itself involved in a formal siege.)

It was not long, however, before British siege and heavy brigades began to find their way to the Western Front. The first siege brigades were sent over in September 1914, just in time for the onset of positional warfare. The first heavy brigades were those that accompanied the 7th and 8th Divisions in October and November 1914. Each of these divisions, which lacked both 60-pdr heavy guns and 4.5in. howitzers, was given a brigade of eight 4.7in. guns as a sort of consolation prize. (Each of these heavy brigades consisted of a headquarters, two heavy batteries and two ammunition columns.) By the middle of 1915, a combined total of 30 siege and heavy brigades were serving with British Empire forces in France and Flanders.

The small number of siege and heavy brigades that served with the Expeditionary Force in the autumn of 1914 was, for the most part, employed as 'GHQ Artillery'. That is, they were permanently assigned to the General Headquarters of the Expeditionary Force itself and lent to various army corps and divisions for specific operations. On 30 March 1915, after the number of

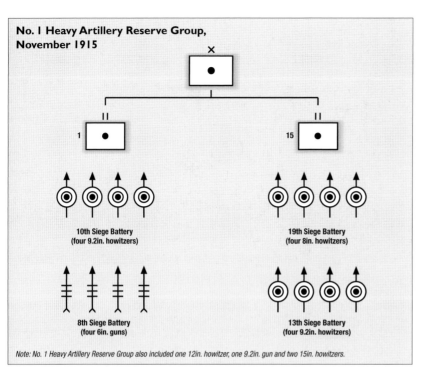

No. 1 Heavy Artillery Reserve Group, November 1915

×

1 ●

15 ●

10th Siege Battery
(four 9.2in. howitzers)

19th Siege Battery
(four 8in. howitzers)

8th Siege Battery
(four 6in. guns)

13th Siege Battery
(four 9.2in. howitzers)

Note: No. 1 Heavy Artillery Reserve Group also included one 12in. howitzer, one 9.2in. gun and two 15in. howitzers.

siege and heavy brigades on the Western Front had grown considerably, they were divided between the Heavy Artillery Reserve and the Army Artillery. The former reported directly to General Headquarters, the latter was divided between the two component armies of the Expeditionary Force.

The Heavy Artillery Reserve was divided into two groups, each of which initially consisted of a single siege brigade and a group headquarters. (The siege brigade was made up of two batteries – one of 6in. guns and one of 9.2in. howitzers.) As more siege batteries joined the Expeditionary Force, the number of units in each group of the Heavy Artillery Reserve grew. In anticipation of this growth, each group was, from the start, commanded by a brigadier-general and provided with a staff comparable to that of the divisional field artillery of an infantry division.

Where the Heavy Artillery Reserve consisted entirely of siege artillery units, the Army Artillery included both siege brigades and heavy brigades. In addition to this, units of the Heavy Artillery Reserve were armed with weapons that were substantially heavier than those of the Army Artillery. That is, the three weapons employed by the siege and heavy brigades of the Army Artillery – the 60-pdr heavy gun, the 4.7in. heavy gun and the 6in. light field howitzer – were all light enough to be pulled by teams of horses. The many weapons employed by the units of the Heavy Artillery Reserve – the smallest of which was the 6in. gun – were either pulled by mechanical tractors or mounted on railway carriages.

At the end of May 1915, a modification of this arrangement maintained the distinction between the Heavy Artillery Reserve and Army Artillery. The Army Artillery, however, was redefined as a collection of horse-drawn siege and heavy brigades that would 'normally be allotted to corps'. At the same time, two new groups were added to the Heavy Artillery Reserve. These new groups were assigned, at a rate of one group per army, to each of the two numbered armies of the Expeditionary Force. In other words, the Army Artillery became 'corps artillery', part of the Heavy Artillery Reserve became 'army artillery' and the other part of the Heavy Artillery Reserve remained 'GHQ artillery'. (In November 1915, after a fifth group of the Heavy Artillery Reserve had been formed to accommodate the Third Army, the groups of the Heavy Artillery Reserve

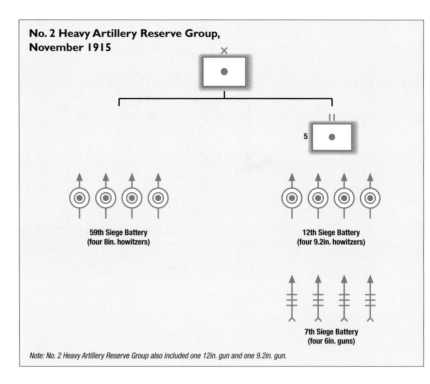

No. 2 Heavy Artillery Reserve Group, November 1915

59th Siege Battery
(four 8in. howitzers)

5

12th Siege Battery
(four 9.2in. howitzers)

7th Siege Battery
(four 6in. guns)

Note: No. 2 Heavy Artillery Reserve Group also included one 12in. gun and one 9.2in. gun.

assigned to numbered armies became the First Army Artillery Group, the Second Army Artillery Group and the Third Army Artillery Group. The same order that implemented this change converted the Army Artillery into Corps Artillery.)

Throughout 1915, the principal building blocks of both the Army Artillery and the Heavy Artillery Reserve were siege brigades and heavy brigades. Consisting of a headquarters, two or three batteries and the ammunition columns belonging to those batteries, these siege and heavy brigades tended to

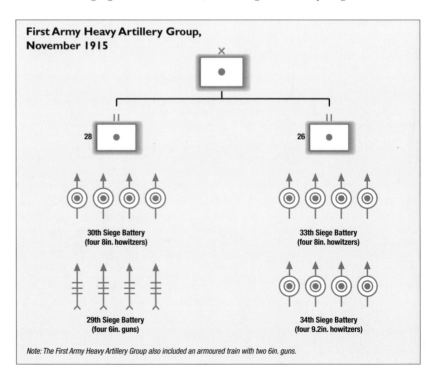

First Army Heavy Artillery Group, November 1915

28

30th Siege Battery
(four 8in. howitzers)

29th Siege Battery
(four 6in. guns)

26

33th Siege Battery
(four 8in. howitzers)

34th Siege Battery
(four 9.2in. howitzers)

Note: The First Army Heavy Artillery Group also included an armoured train with two 6in. guns.

When armed with relatively light weapons (such as 6in. howitzers), siege batteries were usually employed as complete units. When armed with heavier weapons (such as the 9.2in. howitzers shown in this picture), they were often employed as two-piece sections. (Library of Congress)

be highly unstable units. That is, while the batteries of a field artillery brigade were only taken out of it in extraordinary circumstances, the batteries of siege and heavy brigades often moved from one brigade to another. In some cases, this high degree of turnover converted units that had joined the Expeditionary Force as siege brigades into heavy brigades, and units that had crossed the English Channel as heavy brigades into siege brigades. (There were, however, no brigades that consisted of both heavy batteries and siege batteries. Indeed, all heavy brigades of the Expeditionary Force were uniformly armed, either with 60-pdr guns or 4.7in. guns but never a mixture of both. The same was true with siege brigades consisting of batteries equipped with 6in. howitzers. Batteries armed with 6in. guns, 8in. howitzers and 9.2in. howitzers, however, were usually assigned to 'mixed' siege brigades, while siege batteries armed with heavier weapons were either deployed as independent batteries or individual pieces.)

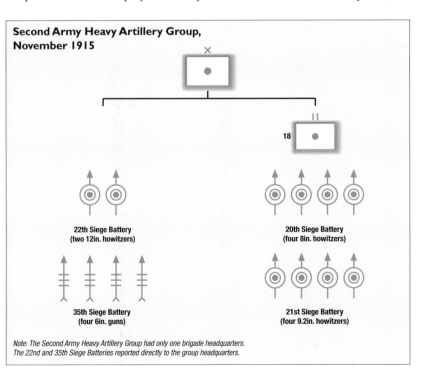

Second Army Heavy Artillery Group, November 1915

22th Siege Battery
(two 12in. howitzers)

20th Siege Battery
(four 8in. howitzers)

35th Siege Battery
(four 6in. guns)

21st Siege Battery
(four 9.2in. howitzers)

Note: The Second Army Heavy Artillery Group had only one brigade headquarters. The 22nd and 35th Siege Batteries reported directly to the group headquarters.

The immediate solution to the problem of the rapid turnover of siege and heavy batteries was a reduction in the use of the terms 'siege brigade' and 'heavy brigade'. Brigades consisting of either siege or heavy batteries became, for many purposes, simply known as 'brigades, Royal Garrison Artillery'. (It is interesting to note that brigades often referred to themselves as siege brigades or heavy brigades long after higher headquarters had abandoned such terminology. It is also worth noting that this new system of nomenclature coincided with the replacement of Roman numerals with Hindu-Arabic ones. Thus, I Siege Brigade and III Heavy Brigade became 1st Brigade, Royal Garrison Artillery and 3rd Brigade, Royal Garrison Artillery.)

Heavy artillery groups

By the spring of 1916, the creation of headquarters for 'brigades, Royal Garrison Artillery' was not keeping up with the production of siege and heavy batteries. That is to say, rather than forming a brigade headquarters for every two or three siege or heavy batteries, the British Army was only producing one brigade headquarters for every six or seven new batteries. Because of this, the ratio of batteries to brigade headquarters was rising so rapidly that the Expeditionary Force faced the spectre of a large number of 'orphan' siege and heavy batteries. This, in turn, promised to put a very large burden on the small headquarters that managed the numbered groups of the Heavy Artillery Reserve, the army artillery groups and the corps artillery establishments.

As was the case with the rest of the Royal Regiment of Artillery at this point in the war, the difficulty lay in the provision of a sufficient number of qualified officers. In particular, there was a dearth of lieutenant-colonels able to command brigades and a shortage of the sort of captain capable of serving in the highly demanding post of brigade adjutant. (Like field artillery brigades, the brigades of the Royal Garrison Artillery were not normally provided with seconds-in-command.)

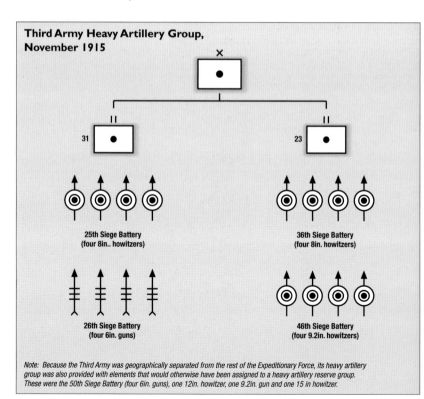

Third Army Heavy Artillery Group, November 1915

31

23

25th Siege Battery
(four 8in.. howitzers)

36th Siege Battery
(four 8in. howitzers)

26th Siege Battery
(four 6in. guns)

46th Siege Battery
(four 9.2in. howitzers)

Note: Because the Third Army was geographically separated from the rest of the Expeditionary Force, its heavy artillery group was also provided with elements that would otherwise have been assigned to a heavy artillery reserve group. These were the 50th Siege Battery (four 6in. guns), one 12in. howitzer, one 9.2in. gun and one 15 in howitzer.

In April 1916, the Expeditionary Force solved its part of this dilemma by converting all of its 'brigades, Royal Garrison Artillery' into 'heavy artillery groups'. Rather than providing direction and support to two or three siege or heavy batteries, these new units used the same headquarters to manage four or five component batteries. These batteries, moreover, were no longer expected to be uniformly armed in the manner of the old heavy brigades or 6in. howitzer siege brigades. Instead, they were deemed capable of handling whatever combination of different types of batteries that the tactical situation required.

Like many British heavy guns of World War I, the 6in. gun was a naval piece that had been adapted for military purposes – first as a coastal defence gun and then as weapon of land warfare. (Library of Congress)

Horse artillery brigades

The single cavalry division of the original Expeditionary Force was provided with two horse artillery brigades. As this division had four cavalry brigades and each horse artillery brigade had two batteries, this arrangement resulted in the provision of a horse artillery battery for each cavalry brigade. Within two months of mobilization, however, three smaller divisions had replaced the single large cavalry division of the Expeditionary Force. As each of these new cavalry divisions had three cavalry brigades, the organizational structure of horse artillery brigades no longer matched that of the arm they existed to support.

The first solution to this structural mismatch was to assign horse artillery batteries directly to cavalry brigades. This facilitated both the separate

Table 14: Personnel of a horse artillery brigade		
	'Square' 1914	'Triangular' 1916
Brigade headquarters	5 officers, 39 other ranks	3 officers, 29 other ranks
Horse artillery battery	5 officers, 200 other ranks	5 officers, 201 other ranks
Horse artillery battery	5 officers, 200 other ranks	5 officers, 201 other ranks
Horse artillery battery	NA	5 officers, 201 other ranks
Headquarters of the ammunition column	2 officers, 11 other ranks	2 officers, 11 other ranks
Ammunition section	1 officer, 106 other ranks	1 officer, 94 other ranks
Ammunition section	1 officer, 106 other ranks	1 officer, 94 other ranks
Ammunition section	NA	1 officer, 94 other ranks
Total	19 officers, 662 other ranks	23 officers, 925 other ranks

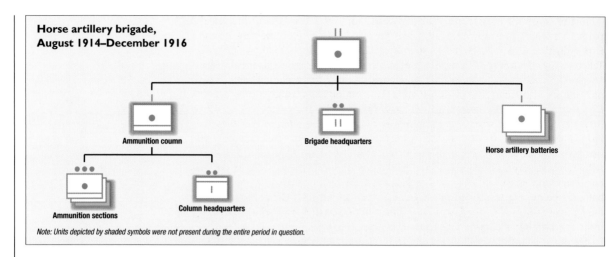

Horse artillery brigade, August 1914–December 1916

Ammunition coumn

Brigade headquarters

Horse artillery batteries

Ammunition sections

Column headquarters

Note: Units depicted by shaded symbols were not present during the entire period in question.

employment of these brigades and the movement of cavalry brigades between divisions. It greatly complicated, however, the relationship between horse artillery batteries and the ammunition columns that kept them supplied with ammunition. That is, each ammunition column had been expressly designed to meet the ammunition needs of a two-battery horse artillery brigade and was thus too small to keep three horse artillery batteries properly supplied.

The second solution to the structural imbalance between horse artillery brigades and the new cavalry divisions was to convert both horse artillery brigades and their component ammunition columns into triangular organizations. This reform, which was implemented in the winter of 1915, affiliated the three horse artillery batteries of each cavalry division with a single horse artillery brigade headquarters and provided a third section for each horse artillery ammunition column. At the same time, the headquarters of the single horse artillery brigade in each cavalry division took over the functions of the headquarters of the divisional artillery. This made possible the dissolution of the latter type of headquarters and the consequent streamlining of the chain of command of the cavalry division.

While this reform had a profound effect upon the size of horse artillery brigades and their component ammunition columns, it wrought very few changes to the brigade headquarters. The most important of these was the elimination of medical and veterinary officers that had originally been attached to each horse artillery brigade. As horse artillery batteries were co-located with cavalry brigades, the medical and veterinary officers of those formations covered the job of caring for the medical needs of both men and horses. Likewise, as the ammunition column was usually in the vicinity of the divisional trains, it was able to make use of the medical and veterinary facilities of that organization.

Field batteries

The British Army that mobilized for World War I had four types of field artillery batteries – six-piece field gun batteries armed with 18-pdr guns, six-piece field howitzer batteries armed with 4.5in. howitzers, four-piece field gun batteries armed with 15-pdr BLC guns, and four-piece howitzer batteries armed with 5in. howitzers. (The first two types of batteries belonged to the Regular Army, the second two belonged to the Territorial Force.) In November 1914, the formation of the 27th and 28th Divisions led to a fifth type of battery – the four-piece field gun battery armed with 18-pdr guns. Two months later, the decision to provide all New Army divisions with four-piece batteries added a sixth type of battery – the four-piece field howitzer battery armed with 4.5in. howitzers. By the middle of 1915, all six of these battery types were serving on the Western Front.

In the course of the second year of World War I, the War Office took great pains to reduce the number of different types of field artillery battery in the Expeditionary Force. The first step towards this goal was a relatively small one. Taken in the autumn of 1915, it involved the replacement of the 216 obsolescent 15-pdr BLC guns then serving with Territorial Force field gun batteries in France or Flanders with factory-fresh 18-pdr guns. The second step, which took place in December 1915 and January 1916, was smaller still. It swapped the 48 old 5in. howitzers of the 12 Territorial Force field howitzer batteries then on the Western Front for new 4.5in. howitzers. The third step, however, was as ambitious as the first two had been modest. It required that all of the four-piece field gun and field howitzer batteries then serving with the Expeditionary Force be either converted into six-piece batteries or dissolved. As all but 70 of the 548 field batteries belonging the Expeditionary Force were armed with either four 18-pdr field guns or four 4.5in. howitzers, this reform subjected the vast majority of such units then on the Western Front to radical surgery.

The most important motive behind the application of the six-piece standard to all of the field artillery batteries of the Expeditionary Force was a desire to economize on officers. In particular, the British Army needed experienced commanders for the many siege artillery, trench mortar and anti-aircraft artillery units it was forming at the time. (Between August 1915 and August 1916, the British Army had formed 166 new siege batteries, some 100 new trench mortar batteries, and 30 or so anti-aircraft batteries.) The disbanding of a third of the New Army and Territorial Force batteries on the Western Front filled nearly all of these billets by making available more than 300 suitable officers – men who had either served as commanding officers or seconds-in-command of field batteries. (The rest of the vacant positions were filled by officers made redundant by similar reforms in other theatres, officers provided by coastal defence companies, and officers who had previously served in horse artillery or heavy batteries.)

As was the case with so many of the organizational reforms that took place in 1916, the creation of mixed field artillery brigades and the abolition of the four-piece field artillery battery did much to reduce old distinctions. Prior to 1916, all field artillery batteries, and nearly all field artillery brigades, were clearly identified as Regular Army, Territorial Force or New Army units. By the start of 1917, most field artillery brigades on the Western Front, as well as a substantial portion of their component batteries, were of mixed ancestry.

Horse artillery batteries

A battery of the Royal Horse Artillery was an artillery unit that, thanks to an extraordinarily generous allocation of riding horses, draught horses and ammunition wagons, could travel at a higher rate of speed than an ordinary field battery. Though these measures allowed a horse artillery battery to keep up with fast-moving cavalry formations, they gave it a substantially larger administrative footprint than a field artillery battery of comparable size. At the same time, the fact that horse artillery batteries were armed with a particularly light field gun (the 13-pdr gun) meant that they had less in the way of firepower than garden-variety field batteries. In other words, horse artillery batteries were well suited to the requirements of mobile warfare but poorly suited to service in the trenches.

During the middle years of the war on the Western Front, horse artillery batteries serving with the Expeditionary Force often found themselves in the uncomfortable position of having far too little to do. As any old soldier might have predicted, this sort of conspicuous idleness led quickly to employment of the sub-optimum sort. Horse artillery batteries thus became the small change of the artillery park, a means of adding a little firepower to one division without borrowing field batteries from another. A notable exception to this rule is provided by the case of the four batteries of Royal Horse

Artillery that were permanently assigned (at a rate of two batteries per division) to the 7th and 8th Divisions. Initially assigned as temporary substitutes for absent field artillery batteries, these batteries retained their 13-pdr horse artillery guns for most of the first year of the war. In the spring of 1915, however, they exchanged their 13-pdrs for 18-pdrs. In doing so, they became field artillery batteries in all but name.

A similar fate befell many of the Territorial Force horse artillery batteries that were sent out to the Middle East during the first year of the war and brought back to Europe in the spring of 1916. As Yeomanry regiments were dismounted in order to provide additional foot soldiers for the Gallipoli campaign, the horse artillery batteries sent out with them were converted into field batteries. At first, this was merely a matter of replacing the lighter horse artillery pieces with full-size field pieces. By the time that these batteries reported for duty on the Western Front, however, their transformation into field artillery units was complete.

Heavy batteries
Prior to 1914, mobile heavy batteries were the premier heavy artillery units of the British Army. In the years between the end of the Second Boer War (1899–1902) and the start of World War I, the British Army raised 22 new heavy batteries – 14 for the Territorial Force, six for the Expeditionary Force and two for the Indian Army. This raised the total number of such units to 26. In the same period, the British Army actually reduced, from 11 to eight, the number of mobile siege batteries that it planned to form upon mobilization. (Two of these units served with the Indian Army. The remaining six were to be formed upon mobilization by the three siege companies serving in the British Isles. All eight of these units, which were known as 'medium siege batteries', were armed with 6in. howitzers.)

During the first few months of World War I, it looked as if the mobile heavy battery would retain its favoured position. Though the 60-pdr heavy gun with which the six Regular Army heavy batteries were armed proved difficult to move and easy to break, it was the only artillery piece in the arsenal of the original Expeditionary Force that could out-range the most common (and most troublesome) heavy piece in the German arsenal – the 150mm heavy field howitzer. Because of this, all 15 of the mobile units raised by the Royal Garrison Artillery between the completion of planned mobilization and the end of 1914 were configured as mobile heavy batteries. (As 60-pdrs were not available, these units – No. 109 Heavy Battery through No. 123 Heavy Battery – were all armed with 4.7in. guns.)

Once the Expeditionary Force began to attack well-fortified positions, heavy batteries lost much of their appeal. The long-range heavy field guns with which they were armed were poorly suited to the definitive tasks of tearing up trenches with high explosive shells, cutting barbed wire with shrapnel, and silencing well-hidden German artillery batteries. In the case of the 4.7in. gun, this problem was made worse by the twin defects of rapid barrel wear and

Table 15: Heavy batteries and siege batteries, August 1914–August 1916						
	Mobilized Aug 1914	Deployed with the original Expeditionary Force	Formed between 1 Sep 1914 and 31 Dec 1914	Serving on the Western Front on 31 Dec 1914	Serving on the Western Front on 1 Aug 1915	Serving on the Western Front on 1 Aug 1916
Heavy batteries	20	6	15	16	32	62
Siege batteries	8	0	0	8	23	132

faulty ammunition. Even the 60-pdr, however, suffered from the inherent inability of all high-velocity weapons to hit point targets that lacked a pronounced vertical face.

Though these problems failed to stop the creation of new heavy batteries, they reversed the relationship between heavy batteries and siege batteries. Before the onset of siege warfare, heavy batteries had been the general-purpose heavy artillery of the British Army and siege batteries had been highly specialized units that were only employed in specific circumstances. By the middle of 1916, the heavy howitzer had become the jack-of-all-trades of the British Army's heavy artillery while the 4.7in. gun and 60-pdr had been demoted to the status of specialized weapons. In particular, heavy batteries were increasingly associated with the mission of long-range interdiction – sending shells into the area behind the German trenches in order to hinder the flow of supplies and reinforcements.

Within heavy batteries, the most important change that took place during the first half of 1916 was the policy of arming all newly formed heavy batteries with 60-pdr guns. This policy, which was put into effect in May of that year, caused a steady rise in the number of 60-pdr guns serving with the Expeditionary Force, from 72 on 1 January 1916 to 360 on 30 December 1916. One month later, the Expeditionary Force began to replace the old 4.7in. guns then serving on the Western Front with new 60-pdrs. However, as newly formed batteries were at the head of the queue for 60-pdrs, most of the older heavy batteries could not be re-armed until well into 1917.

In the autumn of 1916, the Expeditionary Force began to disband some heavy batteries then serving on the Western Front in order to convert others into six-gun units. As was the case with the reform of field batteries that was also taking place at this time, the process of conversion usually involved the attachment of a complete two-gun section from a disbanded battery to a four-gun battery that had escaped that fate. In this way, gun teams that had worked together for a very long time remained intact.

The joining of two-gun sections to four-gun batteries took place without reference to the origins of the units involved. Thus, elements from the Regular Army, the New Armies and the Territorial Force were mixed and matched in every conceivable way, thereby drawing many heavy batteries into the great melting pot that, in the course of 1916, deprived so many units of an exclusive connection to one of the well-defined contingents of the first year of the war.

Siege batteries

Of the five types of artillery battery fielded by the British Army at the start of World War I, the one that was most often replicated in the first two years of the war was the siege battery. In August 1914, the British Army mobilized six siege batteries. In August 1916, it possessed 221 units of that type. To put it mildly, the siege batteries of the British Army multiplied at a rate that would have put rabbits to shame. (The prize for a distant second went to heavy batteries. While the number of siege batteries grew by a factor of nearly 37 in the first 24 months of the war, the number of field batteries grew by a factor of 5.)

What was true for the British Army as a whole was also true for the Expeditionary Force. When the Expeditionary Force was mobilized for active service on 5 August 1914, it contained no siege batteries at all. (Six siege batteries were mobilized by the British Army at this time but were not included in the deployment plan for the Expeditionary Force.) By the first anniversary of mobilization, 26 siege batteries were serving with the Expeditionary Force. By the second anniversary of mobilization, this number had grown to 132.

The weapon most commonly employed by siege batteries was the 6in. howitzer. All six of the original siege batteries had been armed with this weapon, as were ten of the siege batteries serving with the Expeditionary Force in August 1915, and 52 of those deployed on the Western Front in August of 1916. Until the middle of 1915, all of the 6in. howitzers deployed on the Western Front were of a model adopted in the 1890s – the '6in. 30cwt 'of 1896. In the summer of 1915, 6in. howitzers of a very different type – the '6in. 26cwt' – joined these obsolete pieces. Notwithstanding its old-fashioned nomenclature, the 6in. 26cwt howitzer was a true quick-firing artillery piece, with a superb recoil-absorbing mechanism and a rate of fire that was easily twice that of its older counterpart.

Most siege batteries, however, were armed with pieces other than 6in. howitzers. The vast majority of these were new pieces that had been manufactured (and, in some cases, even designed) during the war. The 9.2in. howitzer, which was the second most common siege artillery piece in the middle years of the war, had been adopted in June 1914. Thus, all but the original prototypes were built after the start of the war. The 12in. howitzer and the various 8in. howitzers were all wartime designs. Some of the earlier marks of 6in. gun, however, had existed before the war.

Anti-aircraft batteries

In the years immediately prior to World War I, the design of anti-aircraft weapons progressed even more quickly than the design of aircraft themselves. One reason for this was that the long barrels, flexible mountings and powerful recoil mechanisms needed by such weapons had already been developed for naval purposes. Another was the fact that, even before heavier-than-air aircraft had begun to fly, armies had begun to worry about the problem of balloons. In particular, soldiers throughout Europe were intrigued by the possibility of using lorry-mounted artillery pieces as a means of defending rear areas against hostile balloons.

Despite this rapid progress in the realm of technology, the original Expeditionary Force had no dedicated anti-aircraft weapons of any description. In September 1914, the War Office made its first attempt to remedy this defect by creating a number of independent anti-aircraft detachments armed with Maxim pom-pom guns. As these proved disappointing in action, the War Office made a second attempt to provide British forces on the Western Front with adequate anti-aircraft artillery. This took the form of standard field guns (one 18-pdr and several 13-pdrs) that had been taken off of their field carriages and mounted on naval-type pedestal mounts. Of these, the 13-pdrs, with their particularly long barrels, relatively light shells, and high rates of fire, proved extremely well suited to the task of creating lots of little explosions in the sky. The 13-pdr, which underwent a number of design changes in the course of the war, thus became the standard anti-aircraft gun of the Expeditionary Force for the rest of the war.

The unit of account for British anti-aircraft artillery on the Western Front was the section. This was a fully motorized unit that consisted of a small headquarters, two lorry-mounted anti-aircraft guns and an ammunition lorry. Despite its small size, the anti-aircraft section was designed to be employed as an independent unit. For that reason, it was usually commanded by a captain or a major.

In a few cases, pairs of anti-aircraft sections that were operating in close proximity to each other were combined to form anti-aircraft batteries. These, which were commanded by the senior of the two section

This drawing from a popular wartime magazine shows one of the earliest versions of the 13-pdr anti-aircraft gun. This weapon was created by providing standard 13-pdr field guns with a second set of recoil springs (to compensate for the effects of gravity when firing at high angles) and placing them on a simple pedestal mount. (Great War in a Different Light)

The War Illustrated, May 27th, 1916.

Does Germany Want Peace? By F. A. McKenzie

Regd. as Newspaper & for Canadian Magazine Post.

The War Illustrated

2D Weekly

Vol. 4   Hostile Aeroplane Sighted! Anti-Aircraft Gun in Action in France   No. 93

commanders, took the number of the senior anti-aircraft section taking part in the merger. Thus, when the 40th Anti-Aircraft Section and the 65th Anti-Aircraft Section were assembled into a new battery, the resulting unit was known as the 40th Anti-Aircraft Battery. (This particular merger took place on 1 August 1916.)

In the autumn 1916, the great increase in the number of anti-aircraft sections operating in France led to the creation of substantially larger batteries. These, which were known by letters of the alphabet, consisted of four or more standard sections. (M Anti-Aircraft Battery, for example, consisted of the 40th, 65th, 83rd and 84th Anti-Aircraft Sections.)

In June 1916, the anti-aircraft units – whether batteries or independent sections – operating within the boundaries of each numbered army of the Expeditionary Force were placed under the supervision of anti-aircraft groups. (At this time, an additional anti-aircraft group was formed to provide an organizational home for the anti-aircraft units serving in areas under the jurisdiction of the Lines of Communication organization of the Expeditionary Force.) Commanded by lieutenant-colonels, anti-aircraft groups were modular organizations that had more in common with heavy artillery groups rather than the infantry battalions, field artillery brigades or cavalry regiments of the day. That is to say, they were collections of independently operating tactical units rather than tactical units in their own right. The composition of anti-aircraft groups, moreover, was highly variable. As sections or batteries moved from the sector of one army to that of another, they detached from one group and joined another.

Whether numbered sections, numbered batteries or lettered batteries, all anti-aircraft units of the Expeditionary Force were formed by the depots of the Royal Garrison Artillery. This affiliation provided a number of advantages. Measures taken before the war to protect coastal fortifications against hostile airships gave quite a few members of that branch a certain degree of familiarity with the problem of shooting at aircraft. Similarly, the fact that most of the other duties of the Royal Garrison Artillery (particularly siege warfare and shooting at moving ships) required knowledge of 'scientific gunnery' made it relatively easy for garrison gunners to develop and refine the highly abstract techniques of target engagement required for successful anti-aircraft work. Finally, the fact that most pre-war members of the Royal Garrison Artillery had little experience with horses made them much more suitable for service with fully motorized anti-aircraft units than with horse-drawn artillery units of other kinds.

The 13-pdr 9cwt anti-aircraft gun, which began to arrive on the Western Front in the winter of 1916, was much more powerful than the converted horse artillery pieces issued in 1914 and 1915. Based on the 18-pdr field gun t achieved high muzzle velocity by combining a relatively large propellant cartridge with a relatively small shell. (Library of Congress)

Trench mortar batteries

The trench mortar was the child of the Russo-Japanese War (1904–05), a struggle that provided a preview of the kind of trench warfare that would later take place on the Western Front. In that war, Japanese soldiers looking for ways of dropping explosives onto Russians taking shelter in nearby trenches made a variety of short-range howitzers for themselves. (One of the more interesting models was made mostly of bamboo.) In the years between the end of the Russo-Japanese War and the start of World War I, a number of armies, including that of British-ruled India, conducted extensive experiments with trench mortars. The only army to embrace the weapon on a large scale, however, was the German Army, which provided well-built trench mortars in a variety of sizes to its pioneer battalions.

Though initially designed for the very specific task of creating lanes in barbed-wire obstacles, German trench mortars quickly proved themselves useful in nearly every aspect of positional warfare, from routine harassing fire to local attacks aimed at the capture of specific bits of ground. As might be expected, this encouraged a number of British units to return the compliment by improvising trench mortars of their own. The first of these enterprises, which was launched towards the end of November 1914 by artillery officers of the 8th Division, used smoothbore muzzle-loading mortars that had been designed in the 1830s, built in the 1840s and may well have seen service during the Crimean War. Subsequent experiments used improved versions of these, weapons sent out by the War Office for testing in the field and locally made devices of various sorts.

The first half of 1915 saw the systematic manufacture of trench mortars in workshops belonging to the Expeditionary Force, the beginnings of serial production of such weapons in the United Kingdom and the formation of 35 provisional trench mortar units. (The officers and men of these units came from a variety of sources, including the Royal Engineers, the Royal Horse Artillery and the Royal Garrison Artillery.) By August 1915, the number of British 'trench howitzer batteries' (as they were sometimes known) on the Western Front had risen to 60, the organization of such units had been standardized and the manufacture of various standard models in the United Kingdom had progressed to a point where the workshops of the Expeditionary Force could get out of the business of making trench mortars.

Table 16: War establishments of trench mortar batteries, September 1916			
	Light	Medium	Heavy
Captain	1	0	1
Subalterns	3	2	2
Fitter	0	0	1
Sergeants	2	1	3
Corporals	8	4	8
Gunners	32	16	47
Orderlies	0	0	2
Clerk	0	0	1
Cook	0	0	1
Bâtmen	4	2	3
Total	50	25	69

Note: As the 'gunners' of the light trench mortar batteries were drawn from the infantry battalions of their parent brigades, they bore the rank of 'private'. Similarly, the 'corporals' of medium and heavy trench mortar batteries bore the rank of 'bombardier'.

For most of 1915, the particular model of trench mortar carried by a trench mortar battery had no effect upon the way it was assigned. Whether armed with a spigot mortar that threw a bomb the size of a football or a 'bomb-inside-the-tube' weapon that fired much smaller projectiles, all trench mortar batteries were numbered in the same series, and, while theoretically the property of the Expeditionary Force as a whole, were usually attached to particular divisions on a more-or-less permanent basis.

In November 1915, however, the 'one-size-fits-all' approach to the management of trench mortar units began to change. In that month, the War Office and the General Headquarters of the Expeditionary Force agreed that batteries armed with light ('bomb-inside-the-tube') trench mortars should be assigned to infantry brigades while those equipped with medium and heavy trench mortars (including existing spigot mortars and a number of weapons then being developed) should become divisional assets. This same agreement set the rather ambitious goal of providing each infantry brigade with two light trench mortar batteries and each infantry division with three medium batteries and one heavy battery. In December 1915, a second agreement stipulated that the personnel of light trench mortar batteries were to come from infantry regiments while those of medium and heavy batteries were to come from the Royal Field Artillery. Thus, by a stroke of the pen, the three organizations that had played the largest role in the formation of first trench mortar units – the Royal Engineers, Royal Garrison Artillery and Royal Horse Artillery – were taken out of the trench mortar business.

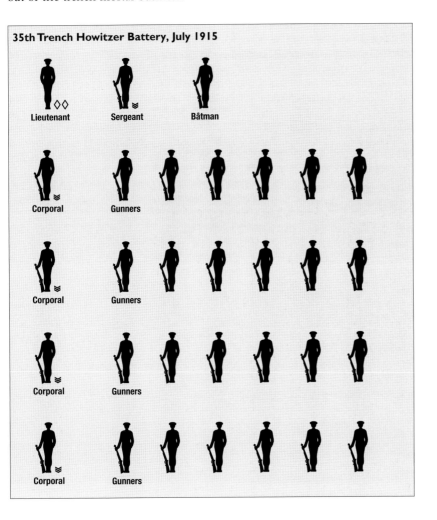

35th Trench Howitzer Battery, July 1915

Lieutenant   Sergeant   Bâtman

Corporal   Gunners

Corporal   Gunners

Corporal   Gunners

Corporal   Gunners

In the course of the winter and spring of 1916, most infantry brigades of the Expeditionary Force managed to obtain two light trench mortar batteries. (A few of these were pre-existing units assigned to the brigades. Most were new units created by drawing men from the infantry battalions of the brigade in question and sending them to a course at a trench mortar school.) At the same time that this was going on, divisions were receiving their medium and heavy batteries. These, too, were a combination of pre-existing trench howitzer batteries that were converted into divisional trench mortar batteries and new units that were 'cut from whole cloth'. (As a rule, the provision of medium trench mortar batteries tended to precede the assignment of heavy trench mortar batteries. Thus, while most divisions possessed their full allotment of three medium trench mortar batteries by the summer of 1916, some had to wait until the winter of 1917 to get their heavy trench mortar units.)

As the widespread employment of trench mortars was seen as a response to a temporary situation, there was no attempt to form the men of trench mortar batteries into a separate regiment on the model of the recently established Machine Gun Corps. Instead, the personnel of trench mortar units remained members of their original regiments, with every expectation of a return to 'real soldiering' once trench warfare had run its course. The same close connection with trench warfare kept the writers of war establishments from providing trench mortar units with much in the way of organic transport. That is to say, where a significant proportion of the men of field artillery units – the drivers, shoeing smiths, wheelers and farriers – were primarily concerned with the horses that moved the guns rather than the guns themselves, nearly all of the men of trench mortar units were members of trench mortar crews. This lack of a transport capability, in turn, made trench mortar batteries much smaller than they might otherwise have been. (A glimpse of what a fully mobile trench mortar battery might have looked like is provided by a proposed establishment submitted by the headquarters of the Second Army on 21 April 1915. Had it been formed, this unit would have had two officers and 59 men.)

Soon after dividing responsibility for trench mortar batteries between infantry brigades and the Royal Field Artillery, the Expeditionary Force rationalized its system of nomenclature for such units. The light trench mortar batteries were given numbers that corresponded to the number of the brigade in which they served. Thus, one trench mortar battery of the 152nd (1st Highland) Infantry Brigade became 152/1 Trench Mortar Battery and the other became 152/2 Trench Mortar Battery. The medium trench mortar batteries were known by a combination of the three last letters of the alphabet and the number of the division. Thus, the first medium trench mortar battery in the 51st (Highland) Division became X.51 Trench Mortar Battery, the second become Y.51 Trench Mortar Battery, and the third became Z.51 Trench Mortar Battery. The heavy trench mortar battery in each division was usually known as V Trench Mortar Battery.

The trench howitzer batteries of 1915 were armed with a variable number of weapons of various different sizes. This high degree of organizational diversity was diminished, but not entirely eliminated, by the rationalization of trench mortar organization that took place in the winter and early spring of 1916. Thus, as late as May 1916, some light trench mortar batteries were still employing medium trench mortars and a few medium trench mortar batteries retained possession of light trench mortars. In the second half of 1916, the replacement of older trench mortars by newer models eliminated this mismatch between the various types of trench mortar batteries and the weapons they used.

As soon as they were formed, medium and heavy trench mortar batteries were placed under the direct supervision of the trench mortar officer of each division, who usually bore the rank of captain or major. Though trench mortar officers lacked the means of creating a proper headquarters for such a unit, their

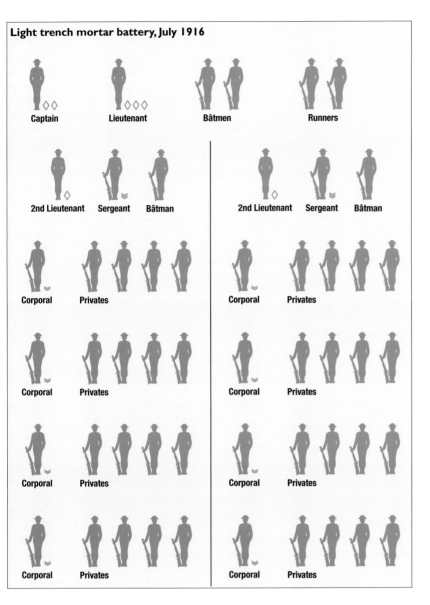

Light trench mortar battery, July 1916

Captain — Lieutenant — Bâtmen — Runners

2nd Lieutenant — Sergeant — Bâtman — 2nd Lieutenant — Sergeant — Bâtman

Corporal — Privates — Corporal — Privates

Corporal — Privates — Corporal — Privates

Corporal — Privates — Corporal — Privates

Corporal — Privates — Corporal — Privates

existence often led to the custom of referring to the medium and trench mortar batteries of each division as a 'trench mortar group' or a 'trench howitzer brigade'. No such arrangements, however, were made for the light trench mortar batteries of infantry brigades. Instead, each one was treated as a completely independent unit that reported directly to the brigade commander in much the same way as an infantry battalion or the machine-gun company. Consequently, any cooperation that took place between the two trench mortar batteries was either the result of mutual agreement between the battery commanders or an artifact of a plan emanating from brigade headquarters. In June and July 1916, this rather awkward situation was remedied by the amalgamation of the two light trench mortar batteries in each infantry brigade into a single eight-piece battery. This unit, which was often called the 'brigade trench mortar battery', was divided into two four-gun sections and bore the number of its parent infantry brigade. Thus, for example, 152/1 and 152/2 Light Trench Mortar Batteries became the 1st and 2nd Sections of the 152nd Light Trench Mortar Battery. (In some batteries, the two sections were styled as the 'Right Half-Battery' and the 'Left Half-Battery' or even just 'Right Half' and 'Left Half'.)

The first establishments promulgated for trench mortar batteries were completely independent of the type of weapon employed. In October 1915, for example, the War Office published a table of organization for a 'trench mortar battery' that could just as easily be equipped with medium spigot mortars as 'bomb-in-the-tube' light mortars. In February 1916, when trench mortar units were divided into 'light' (infantry) and 'medium' (artillery) batteries, this organizational structure was retained by both types of unit. By September 1916, however, the amalgamation of the two light trench mortar batteries in each brigade and the appearance of first heavy trench mortar batteries had created a situation in which there were three distinct establishments for trench mortar units.

Motor machine-gun batteries

Though it may well have been initially inspired by the horse-drawn machine-gun detachments of German cavalry divisions, the motor machine-gun battery was a uniquely British organization that owed its particular form to two somewhat related developments in the civilian economy of the United Kingdom during the years just before World War I. One of these developments was the spectacular rise of the motorcycle, which provided the United Kingdom with dozens of firms that manufactured such devices and scores of thousands of men who were able to operate them. The other development was the rapid drop in the number of light draught horses living in the British Isles. These animals, which had once been the mainstay of the British transportation system, were being quickly replaced by a combination of automobiles and heavy draught horses. As light draught horses were indispensable ingredients of field artillery units, the planners at the War Office were particularly open to proposals that might enhance the firepower of the Expeditionary Force without drawing upon the limited supply of such animals.

In the autumn of 1914, plans for the expansion of the British Army included the creation of a motor machine-gun battery for each infantry division of the Expeditionary Force. By April 1915, however, it became clear that positional warfare was more than a temporary interruption of the war of grand manoeuvres. As a result, the War Office abandoned its plan to provide a motor machine-gun battery to each infantry division. Nonetheless, a total of 15 motor machine-gun batteries managed to cross the English Channel during the first year of the war.

Motor machine-gun batteries spent the second year of World War I in a sort of organizational limbo. In some cases they were attached to divisions, in other cases to army corps. At no time, however, was the motor machine-gun battery made an integral part of any particular formation. As the shortage of machine guns turned into abundance, this put the motor machine-gun batteries in the uncomfortable position of being, in effect, the overstaffed, unattached equivalents of half of an infantry brigade machine-gun company. In the spring of 1916, however, motor machine-gun companies were saved from imminent dissolution by the creation of a 'mounted troops' organization in each army corps. As the number of motor machine-gun batteries was similar to the number of army corps serving with the Expeditionary Force at that time and the other elements of the corps mounted troops were entirely bereft of heavy machine guns, the assignment of a motor machine-gun battery to each army corps killed two birds with one stone. It also got both the bicycle battalions and the cavalry regiments in the habit of working with motorized units and thus brought them a step closer to the role they would often play in the last year of the war.

The structure of the motor machine-gun batteries of 1916 was close to that of the provisional establishment for such units that was laid down in the autumn of 1914. As before, each motor machine-gun battery consisted of a headquarters and three two-gun sections. The changes that did take place included the addition of a third subaltern officer (which allowed the assignment of one such officer to lead each section), the addition of four scouts to the battery headquarters and the replacement of many single-seat motorcycles with two-passenger machines. This latter development allowed three additional machine-gunners to join each section and increased the amount of ammunition that could be carried with the battery. (The standard ammunition load for the battery was 52,000 rounds, with 40,000 rounds being carried in motorcars and 12,000 rounds on the two-passenger motorcycles of the machine-gun sections.)

Table 17: Establishments of machine-gun units, July 1916

	Machine-gun company Headquarters	Machine-gun squadron Headquarters	Motor machine-gun battery Headquarters
Commanding officer	1	1	1
Second-in-command	1	1	0
Sergeant-major	1	1	1
Quartermaster sergeant	1	1	0
Farrier	0	1	0
Transport sergeant	1	0	0
Artificer	1	0	0
Armourer (AOC)	0	1	0
Shoeing smith corporal	0	1	0
Shoeing smith	1	0	0
Saddlers	1	2	0
Saddletree maker	0	1	0
Signaller (corporal)	1	0	0
Signallers	3	4	0
Clerk	0	1	0
Range takers	8	0	0
Scouts	8	0	4
Drivers	3	3	3
Storeman	1	0	0
Cooks	2	0	0
Bâtmen	2	4	1
Water duties (RAMC)	2	2	0
Total for headquarters	38	24	10

	Four sections	Six sections	Three sections
Subalterns	8	6	3
Sergeants	8	6	3
Corporals	8	6	3
Shoeing smith	0	6	0
Fitters	0	0	3
Privates	64	126	32
Drivers	20	36	3
Cooks	0	6	0
Bâtmen	8	12	3
Total for sections	116	204	50
Total for unit	154	228	60

The Royal Engineers

The original Expeditionary Force includes four basic types of engineer units: field units, fortress units, signals units and one-of-a-kind specialized units. Of these, only the field and fortress units performed the sort of tasks that are currently associated with the Royal Engineers. The rest did work that would later be associated with other corps of the British Army – particularly the Royal Corps of Signals and the Royal Electrical and Mechanical Engineers. Nonetheless, it would be a mistake to draw too thick a line between the services performed by 'proper engineers' and those that lay beyond the traditional boundaries of military engineering. This was because the war on the Western Front was, among many other things, an enormously complex technical enterprise that involved not only the application of siegecraft to battle, but the creation and maintenance of a vast infrastructure of headquarters, camps, depots, workshops, aerodromes, roads, railways and communications networks.

Table 18: Non-divisional engineer units of the Expeditionary Force (not including parks, depots and signal units)

Unit	Number serving on 5 August		
	1914	1915	1916
Fortress/army troops companies	1	14	42
Siege companies	0	6	6
Railway companies	0	6	20
Bridging trains/pontoon park companies	2	3	10
Tunnelling companies	0	9	25
Special (gas warfare) companies	0	5	5
Quarrying companies	0	0	2
Land drainage companies	0	0	2
Survey companies	0	0	4
Printing companies	1	1	1
Printing sections	0	2	4
Postal sections	1	1	1
Special works company	1	1	1
Anti-aircraft searchlight sections	0	2	8
Inland water transport sections	0	0	11
Meteorological sections	0	0	1
Artisan works companies	0	0	2
Electrical and mechanical companies	0	0	1

The middle years of the war in France and Flanders saw a great increase in the number of engineer units. A substantial portion of this increase was the inevitable result of the general expansion of the British forces on the Western Front. With each new infantry division, for example, came three field companies and a divisional signal company. Thus, by the second anniversary of the war, 195 field companies and 65 divisional signal companies were serving with the Expeditionary Force. The lion's share of the new engineer units crossing the English Channel, however, were non-divisional units of various kinds. These ranged from close copies of the non-divisional engineer units of the original Expeditionary Force to units of types that had not even been imagined in the years before the war.

Field, army troops and siege companies

In mobile warfare, the Royal Engineer field companies of the Expeditionary Force were primarily concerned with enhancing the mobility of friendly forces and degrading that of the enemy. To that end, much of their work – which included locating fords, building and repairing bridges, destroying bridges and improvising ferry services – was closely tied to the crossing of rivers. In positional warfare, the emphasis of field engineering shifted to the building of shelters, the erection of obstacles, and attempts to improve the inherently difficult living conditions of front-line garrisons. These latter efforts were greatly facilitated by the long-standing (and often criticized) policy of limiting enlistment into the Royal Engineers to men who had passed a 'trades test'. Because of this trades test, the rank-and-file of a field engineering unit was likely to include a number of fully qualified carpenters, bricklayers, masons and ironworkers, as well as men who were intimate with either machinery or electricity.

The onset of trench warfare had a slightly different impact upon the four fortress companies assigned to Expeditionary Force by the deployment plan that was executed in August of 1914. These had been designed for service in permanent fortresses of the traditional type, with duties that included the repair of damage caused by enemy action and the building of supplementary earthworks. Their primary role within the Expeditionary Force, however, was the maintenance of the physical infrastructure of the lines of communications – the roads and bridges that connected the fighting echelon of the Expeditionary Force with the Continental port cities that served as its base. Once mobile warfare gave way to positional warfare, the four original fortress companies, as well as the many fortress companies that came after them, took up duties that bore a close resemblance to the work that they had originally been formed to perform. In particular, they became closely associated with the largely unsung task of building those features of the defensive system that lay behind the forward trenches. These included a second line of defence (the 'corps defence line'), as well as storage

Table 19: War establishments of engineer companies, September 1916			
	Field company	Army troops company	Siege company
Major	1	0	1
Captains	1	1	2
Subalterns	4	2	5
Sergeant-major	1	1	1
Quartermaster sergeant	1	1	1
Interpreter	0	1	0
Sergeants	6	5	11
Farrier sergeant	1	0	0
Shoeing smith	1	1	0
Corporals	7	7	18
2nd corporals	7	8	17
Buglers	0	0	2
Fitters	0	0	2
Sappers	139	102	222
Drivers	38	17	9
Bâtmen	8	3	8
RAMC (water duties)	2	2	0
Total	217	151	299

Table 20: Transport of engineer companies, September 1916

	Field company	Army troops company	Siege company
Draught horses (or mules)	55	18	16
Pack horses (or mules)	4	0	0
Bicycles	0	10	8
Motorcycles (side-car)	0	3	0
Motorcycles (solo)	0	0	8
Motorcar (box body)	0	0	1
Lorries (3-ton)	0	2	4

facilities, gun emplacements, workshops, observation posts, aeroplane hangars and water-supply systems. In addition to this, fortress companies were often employed in maintaining the roads and bridges that led up to the front lines. These, which had mostly been built to meet the relatively modest needs of rural communities in northern France and Flanders, suffered heavily from the unaccustomed burdens of heavy military traffic and German bombardment.

Like fortress companies, the siege companies of the two engineer regiments of the Special Reserve – the Royal Anglesey Royal Engineers and the Royal Monmouthshire Royal Engineers – had originally been designed to take part in fortress warfare of the kind imagined in the years before World War I. In particular, their purpose was to serve either as a reinforcement to the fortresses companies that were helping to defend a British fortress or as part of a force besieging an enemy fortress. Once on the Western Front, the siege companies were employed in much the same way as fortress companies. However, because they were nearly twice as large as fortress companies, siege companies were employed for tasks that were judged suitable for two fortress companies.

In August 1915, the fortress companies of the British Army were officially designated as 'army troops companies'. While this new name diminished the tendency to view fortress companies as being exclusively concerned with defensive siege warfare, it created a new misconception. Though fortress companies were occasionally assigned directly to numbered armies and thus formed part of the army troops of those formations, the vast majority of fortress companies were assigned directly to army corps. The term 'corps troops' companies would thus have been more appropriate. (It is interesting to note that the decision to rename the fortress companies was taken at a time when 'army artillery' was defined as those batteries that were normally assigned to army corps.)

Field, army troops and siege companies were heavily dependent upon other units for the labour needed to complete most construction projects. In the case of the field companies, this labour came from the various fighting units of the infantry divisions and army corps – particularly the infantry brigades, the pioneer battalions and the mounted troops. In addition to this, the many qualified tradesmen serving in the ranks of units other than engineer units were often employed to supplement the skilled work of the Royal Engineers. This was particularly true where carpentry was concerned. (The building and maintenance of trenches, dugouts, walkways and other features of a fortified position consumed immense quantities of wood. To meet this need, many infantry brigades established their own woodworking shops.) In the case of army troops and siege companies, this labour was provided by replacement drafts awaiting transfer to units at the front, military prisoners, convalescents who were not yet fit for service at the front, prisoners of war, regularly constituted labour units and units of the French Army composed of over-age and unfit soldiers. (To assist in communicating with men belonging to the last-named units, each army troops company was provided with an interpreter.)

Anti-aircraft searchlight sections

Prior to World War I, the searchlights of the British Army were the responsibility of the fortress and electric lights companies of the Royal Engineers. (The electric lights companies were Territorial Force units that dealt with the electrical needs of fortresses. The fortress companies were Regular Army units that dealt with all of the engineering needs of fortresses, including those involving electricity.) While some of these electric lights could be pointed to the sky in order to illuminate hostile aircraft, the vast majority were employed as a means of locating enemy warships. To that end, they were, as a rule, employed in the large number of coastal fortifications that guarded the ports, harbours and rivers of the British Isles and, in the case of the Regular Army units, the British Empire as well.

The exclusive connection between searchlights and territorial defence ended in March 1915 when Sir John French, then the Field Marshal Commanding-in-Chief of the Expeditionary Force, asked the War Office for searchlights to assist the anti-aircraft guns that were deployed in the vicinity of his headquarters in order to defend it against attack by German airships. The War Office responded to this request by forming two searchlight sections, each of three searchlights, one officer, one sergeant, one staff sergeant ('mechanist'), and 18 'rank and file'. The first of these sections, No. 1 Anti-Aircraft Searchlight Section, Royal Engineers, was composed of men of the Regular Army. The second, No. 2 Anti-Aircraft Searchlight Section, was made up of a mixture of Regular soldiers and men of the London Electrical Engineers. (The London Electrical Engineers was a six-company unit of the Territorial Force that was recruited largely from men who worked in the electrical trades.)

No. 1 Anti-Aircraft Searchlight Section went to France in April 1915 while No. 2 Section crossed the English Channel three months later. In the year that followed, the London Electrical Engineers cooperated with their sister unit, the Tyne Electrical Engineers, to provide six additional anti-aircraft searchlight sections for the British Expeditionary Force. These were of basically the same type as the first two sections, with three searchlights, one officer (who might

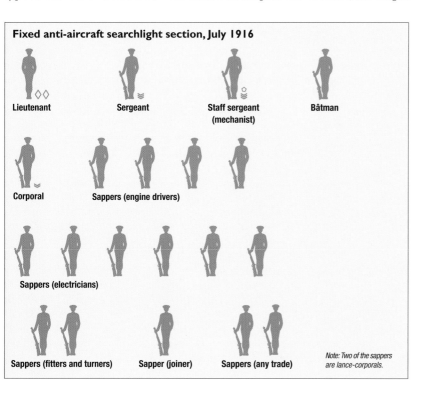

Fixed anti-aircraft searchlight section, July 1916

Lieutenant

Sergeant

Staff sergeant (mechanist)

Bâtman

Corporal

Sappers (engine drivers)

Sappers (electricians)

Sappers (fitters and turners)

Sapper (joiner)

Sappers (any trade)

Note: Two of the sappers are lance-corporals.

be a captain but was usually a lieutenant) and 20 other ranks. In July 1916, however, this establishment was reduced by one searchlight and three men. (One reason for this was a shortage of searchlights. Another was the fact that three searchlights placed around a target formed a convenient aiming point for German aircraft intent upon dropping bombs.) Thus, the seven anti-aircraft searchlight sections sent to the Western Front between August 1916 and January 1917 consisted of one officer, one sergeant, one staff-sergeant, one corporal, two lance-corporals, one driver and 13 sappers.

Ideally, all of the 'other ranks' of each anti-aircraft searchlight section (save the driver, who was seconded from the Army Service Corps) were qualified tradesmen. Specifically, the official establishment for such units called for six electricians, four engine drivers, two fitters and turners, one joiner and one sapper qualified in any recognized trade. By the middle of 1916, however, the enormous expansion of the Royal Engineers had created a shortage of qualified tradesmen. As a result, a proportion of the men assigned to anti-aircraft searchlight sections were 'category B' infantrymen. That is, they were men who had been taken out of their battalions because, while fit enough to serve in rear areas, they had been deemed no longer capable of handling the enormous physical stress of serving in the front lines.

The Army Service Corps

The great expansion of the Expeditionary Force that took place during the first two years of World War I was accompanied by an enormous increase in both the number and the variety of Army Service Corps units serving on the Western Front. The task of making sense of the organization, distribution and functions of these units is greatly complicated by the peculiarities of the nomenclature employed by the writers of war establishments. A 'general headquarters ammunition park', for example, was not, as might be imagined, a static unit assigned directly to the General Headquarters of the Expeditionary Force. Rather, it was a highly mobile unit (with 106 3-ton ammunition lorries) that was normally assigned to an army corps. The 'advanced mechanical transport depot' (nine officers, 254 men) and the 'advanced horse transport depot' (16 officers, 335 men) were similar enough in size to justify the use of the same term to describe both. The 'base mechanical transport depot' (24 officers, 516 men) was, nonetheless, more than eight times as large as the 'base horse transport depot' (five officers, 60 men).

One way to impose a little order on this structural cacophony is to distinguish those units that evolved from the Army Service Corps establishment of the original Expeditionary Force from those that were added during the war. Upon mobilization, the Expeditionary Force was provided with 26 horse-drawn supply and transport companies, eight division supply columns, eight division ammunition parks, six reserve parks and four

By 1916, columns of troops travelling by motor lorry were a common sight in the rear areas of the Western Front. In World War I, all motor vehicle drivers serving in the Expeditionary Force (except members of tank crews and motorcycle riders) were members of the Army Service Corps. (Library of Congress)

'transport depots' of various kinds. Of these, only the horse-drawn supply and transport companies were directly assigned to divisions. (Strictly speaking, four such units formed the division trains of one of the six infantry divisions of the original Expeditionary Force. Of the remaining six supply and transport companies, five were allocated to the Cavalry Division and one was set aside for the support of army troops.) All of the other Army Service Corps units belonged to one of the two rear-area commands of the original Expeditionary Force – the Lines of Communication and the Base.

In the course of the first two years of the war, the army corps took over a number of the logistics functions from the Lines of Communication. The division supply columns and the division artillery parks – so called because they were allocated on the basis of one such unit for each infantry division in the theatre of operations – thus became part of the corps troops establishment of army corps. In the same period, the great increase in the consumption of ammunition led to the addition of a fourth ammunition park to each corps. When these additional ammunition parks, which bore the somewhat confusing designation of 'GHQ ammunition parks', arrived on the Western Front, the 'division artillery parks' were subordinated to them, thereby becoming 'ammunition sub-parks'. The growth of corps heavy artillery establishments led to the creation of organizations known as 'siege parks'. These provided an organizational home for the motor vehicles of the heavy artillery units, as well as for the men who drove and maintained those vehicles.

Apart from these organizations, all other Army Service Corps units were assigned to either the old rear-area commands (which had grown immensely during the first half of the war) or the headquarters of numbered armies. These rear-area and army troops units were of four basic types. Transport depots were concerned with the provision of the means of transportation – whether four legged or motor driven – to other units. Auxiliary companies – which might be equipped with horse-drawn wagons, petrol-driven lorries, steam-driven lorries or double-decker omnibuses – reinforced the transport capabilities of divisional supply columns and the division trains. Supply companies and detachments were static units that were concerned with the storage, organization and issue

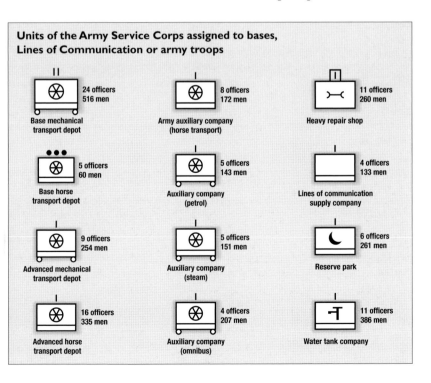

Units of the Army Service Corps assigned to bases, Lines of Communication or army troops

24 officers / 516 men — **Base mechanical transport depot**	8 officers / 172 men — **Army auxiliary company (horse transport)**	11 officers / 260 men — **Heavy repair shop**
5 officers / 60 men — **Base horse transport depot**	5 officers / 143 men — **Auxiliary company (petrol)**	4 officers / 133 men — **Lines of communication supply company**
9 officers / 254 men — **Advanced mechanical transport depot**	5 officers / 151 men — **Auxiliary company (steam)**	6 officers / 261 men — **Reserve park**
16 officers / 335 men — **Advanced horse transport depot**	4 officers / 207 men — **Auxiliary company (omnibus)**	11 officers / 386 men — **Water tank company**

In 1916, the Army Service Corps was in the forefront of the effort to replace horse-drawn vehicles with motorized ones. Nonetheless, members of that corps were still considered 'mounted' troops and were thus often seen wearing spurs, riding breeches, bandoliers and lanyards. (Author's collection)

of the kinds of supplies handled by the Army Service Corps, particularly food, fodder, petrol and supplies associated with mechanical transport. Specialized service units performed the functions described in their titles. Field butcheries cut meat, field bakeries baked bread, and water-tank companies delivered potable water in lorry-mounted water trucks. Heavy- and light-repair shops, however, were not general-purpose repair establishments. Rather, they were exclusively concerned with motor vehicles. (Heavy-repair shops performed extensive repair work. Light-repair shops did jobs that were largely a matter of installing new parts.) Similarly, the 'workshop for six anti-aircraft gun detachments' was exclusively concerned with the maintenance of the lorries upon which anti-aircraft guns were mounted rather than the guns themselves. (That work fell into the bailiwick of the Army Ordnance Corps.)

The Royal Flying Corps

As initially conceived, the aeroplane squadrons of the Royal Flying Corps were instruments of operational reconnaissance. That is, each of the seven original squadrons was to serve as the long-range eyes of an infantry or cavalry division, scouring the countryside for hostile columns and keeping the division commander aware of the location of friendly forces. On the very eve of the war, the aeroplane squadrons took on a second mission – that of artillery observation. As mobile warfare gave way to positional warfare, this second mission began to eclipse the first. At the same time, the desire to figure out what was happening on the other side of no-man's land led to the rapid development of both close reconnaissance and aerial photography.

In the course of the first year of the war, the British Army found it easier to create infantry divisions than aeroplane squadrons. Thus, the ratio of aeroplane squadrons to divisions dropped from 1:1 to 1:3. The logic of this arithmetic was sufficiently powerful to convert the aeroplane squadron from a unit that cooperated with divisions to one that worked closely with army corps. At the same time, the doubling of the number of squadrons deployed with the Expeditionary Force – from six in September 1914 to 12 in September 1915 – created the need for some sort of intermediate headquarters. Thus was born the first two 'wings', which were created in the winter of 1915 to provide an organizational home for the aeroplane squadrons of each numbered army. (As might be expected, the 1st Wing was formed to accommodate the squadrons of the First Army while the 2nd Wing provided the same service to the Second Army.)

In the course of the second year of the war, the number of aeroplanes serving with the Expeditionary Force grew from 125 or so (August 1915) to more than 400 (July 1916). The number of squadrons also grew during this period, but not to the same degree. The chief reason for this lack of proportion was the decision, taken by the War Office in March 1916, to increase the number of aeroplanes in each squadron from 12 to 18. Thus, while the number of aeroplanes grew by a factor of three, the number of squadrons merely doubled.

As the Royal Flying Corps grew, its component elements began to specialize. Some wings continued to work closely with army corps. Others took on such tasks as hunting down hostile aircraft, long-range reconnaissance and aerial bombardment. On 30 January 1916, this division of labour was formalized by the establishment of a 'brigade, Royal Flying Corps' in each field army. Each of these brigades, which bore the number of its affiliated army, consisted of two wings. The first wing, which contained a squadron for each army corps in the field army, became known as the 'corps wing'. The second, which consisted of squadrons equipped with the machines best suited for either air-to-air combat or short-range bombing, became the 'army wing'. (In April 1916, the transfer of all 'fighting' aircraft to the army wings gave them a monopoly on such work.) The wing left over by the formation of brigades was assigned directly to the General Headquarters of the Expeditionary Force, where it specialized in reconnaissance and bombardment at relatively long ranges.

Command, control, communications and intelligence

Where both technology and organization were concerned, the system for command and control of the Expeditionary Force began World War I with a considerable advantage over its counterparts in other armies. The modular organization of signal units, for example, allowed divisions, army corps or armies to custom tailor their communications infrastructure to the situation at hand. In particular, it facilitated an enormous expansion in the use of the telephone. (The signal units of the Expeditionary Force had originally been designed with non-vocal communications in mind. That is to say, wires and cables were, for the most part, provided for use with telegraph devices of various sorts. By the start of 1916, however, these had largely given way to voice telephones.) Similarly, early enthusiasm for portable wireless sets (which was closely associated with the large cavalry component of the Expeditionary Force) gave the Royal Flying Corps considerable edge when it came to air-to-ground communications.

The human element of the command and control system of the Expeditionary Force was, however, much less advanced than either its organization or its equipment. In particular, the Expeditionary Force was plagued by a great deal of uncertainty as to the proper relationship among commanders at various levels. As a result, decisions which should have been left to the discretion of the officers commanding brigades and divisions were often taken by the commanders of armies and army corps while the commanders of armies and army corps often failed to promulgate the sort of guidance that would have allowed subordinates to cooperate in a more effective manner.

The roots of both sets of errors lay in the fact that officers of the pre-war British Army had very little experience with the handling of large units and formations. With infantry battalions, artillery brigades and cavalry regiments scattered all over the globe, the few opportunities that commanders of brigades and divisions had to practise their craft were often devoted to the needs of subordinate units. In some cases, this was done in a very 'hands-off' manner, with the general playing the role of a coach or umpire. In others, generals coped with the inexperience of subordinates by giving highly detailed orders that had to be obeyed to the letter. During the first two years of World War I, both of these tendencies were exaggerated by the rapid growth of the Expeditionary Force. Men who had been competent commanders of relatively small units in the years before the war found themselves dealing with the unfamiliar problems of running a much larger command. In some cases, they dealt with this conundrum by focusing on those duties that they were most comfortable with, even if this meant depriving subordinates of their freedom of action. In other cases, the senior commanders took on the role of indulgent uncles, encouraging and supporting their subordinates while failing to act decisively at the moment of truth.

Intelligence

The two most importance intelligence activities of the Expeditionary Force were the quest to establish the order of battle of the German Army and the programme to assist the counter-battery effort of army corps at the front. Neither of these had little to do with the cloak-and-dagger world of espionage. Instead, each was a mammoth exercise in puzzle solving, an attempt to draw an accurate picture of the situation on the other side of no man's land by

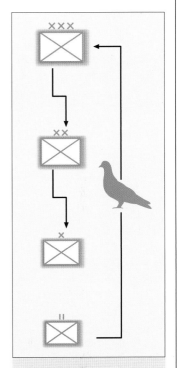

Carrier pigeons and the telephone were not so much competing means of communication as complementary parts of the same system. A pigeon released from a battalion headquarters, for example, would invariably return to his home loft. At that loft, signallers of the corps signal company would recover the message and, using the rear-area telephone network, pass it on to the intended recipient. (This, in most cases, was the headquarters of the brigade to which the originating battalion belonged.) Notwithstanding the many steps involved in this process and the circuitous route taken by each message, the combination of pigeon and telephone was as reliable as the despatch of a runner and often much speedier.

collecting, qualifying, cross-referencing and arranging thousands of discrete pieces of information. Because of this, the people who ran the intelligence apparatus of the Expeditionary Force had much more in common with archaeologists, librarians and archivists than with the dashing heroes of a John Buchan novel.

Until the Russian Revolution of 1917, the chief task of the Franco-British alliance was to keep the largest possible number of German soldiers fighting on the Western Front, thereby preventing the German Army from building a strategic reserve that was powerful enough to knock Russia out of the war. The chief gauge of the effectiveness of French and British efforts was thus less a matter of ground gained, guns captured or men killed. It was the percentage of the German Army that was serving on the Western Front. Determining this number, in turn, required the compilation of an accurate, up-to-date order of battle of both the German Army as a whole and that portion of the German Army that was fighting on the Western Front.

The information of greatest value to order-of-battle intelligence was that which came from prisoners. This included information garnered during interrogation, information provided by items of clothing (such as shoulder straps with regimental numbers on them) and, most important of all, the little pay-book that every German soldier was required to carry on his person at all times. In addition to recording such things as payments made, punishments awarded and promotions, each pay-book contained valuable information about the state of the German training and replacement system. In particular, each pay-book recorded the regimental serial number of the soldier it belonged to. As these serial numbers were sequential, they gave a very good sense of how many men had passed through a given regimental depot at a given time. When combined with serial numbers gleaned from other pay-books, this allowed British intelligence analysts to estimate such things as casualties and the rate at which the German Army was using up its manpower reserves.

For the purposes of order-of-battle intelligence, a large number of prisoners captured in one place was much less valuable than a steady trickle of prisoners from the entire front. As the most important source of such prisoners was trench raiding, intelligence officers became the most vocal advocates of that practice. The kind of raids that intelligence officers preferred, however, were not the large-scale destructive raids recorded in so many divisional histories, but small-scale forays across no man's land in order to snatch a sentry or two.

While order-of-battle intelligence was the handmaiden of strategy, counter-battery intelligence was the servant of tactics. Its purpose was to facilitate the silencing (and, if possible, the destruction) of German artillery batteries by determining their exact location. To this end, counter-battery intelligence made extensive use of aerial reconnaissance, aerial photography and a set of increasingly sophisticated techniques for exploiting the visual and auditory clues that were produced each time that an artillery piece was fired.

Weapons and equipment

As had been the case with the first year of the war, the weapons issued to units of the British Army during the second year of World War I were, on the whole, much better than those given to units of the French and German armies of the day. The basic weapons of the infantry divisions of the original Expeditionary Force – the short Lee-Enfield rifle, the Vickers heavy machine gun, the 18-pdr field gun and the 4.5in. howitzer – retained the considerable advantage over comparable French and German weapons that they had enjoyed from the very start of the war. The 6in. 26cwt. 'Vickers' howitzer that became available in the spring of 1915 and proliferated in 1916 was on a par with its closest competitor – the German 150mm heavy field howitzer of 1913. What was more important, the 'Vickers' was a considerably better artillery piece than its most numerous opposite number, the German 150mm heavy field howitzer of 1902. (The German heavy field howitzers, which fired the 100lb shells that British Empire troops called 'Jack Johnsons' and 'Black Marias', had formed the backbone of the German artillery park in 1914 and would remain in that role until the very end of the war.) The new Lewis light machine gun, which was initially ordered as a second-class substitute for the Vickers gun, was likewise well ahead of its Continental competition. At a time when German light machine guns could only achieve reliability by being extraordinarily heavy and French light machine guns achieved lightness at the expense of reliability, the Lewis was both light and reliable. Indeed, the highest praise for this extraordinary weapon came from the Germans, who re-chambered captured Lewis guns for their own ammunition and issued them to their elite assault battalions. (The regimental history of one of these battalions referred to these weapons as the 'beloved Lewis guns.')

In terms of siege ordnance, the second year of World War I saw the Expeditionary Force take delivery of hundreds of very heavy, and, for the most part, very new, heavy howitzers. The most important of these pieces was the 9.2in. siege howitzer, which had been adopted as the standard weapon of British heavy siege batteries in June 1914. With a shell that weighed nearly three times as much as that of the new 6in. heavy field howitzer, the 9.2in. howitzer proved itself an indispensable means of dealing with the extraordinarily well-built fortified positions that the Germans began to create in the spring of 1915. (These positions, which were characterized by very deep shelters and the extensive use

When first issued to units of the Expeditionary Force, steel helmets were seen as 'trench stores' – items that, like flare pistols and wire cutters, were only used by trench garrisons. By the end of 1916, however, the helmet had become an item of personal issue, a part of the uniform that accompanied a soldier everywhere he went. Easily recognized by its distinctive silhouette, the broad-brimmed 'tin hat' quickly became the surest means of identifying a British soldier at a distance. (Library of Congress)

For most of 1916, the standard web equipment of the British rifleman was still in short supply. As a result, most second-line units, and even a few front-line ones, had to make do with old-fashioned leather equipment. (US National Archives)

of reinforced concrete, were entirely immune to the effects of field artillery and were resistant to damage caused by shells fired by 6in. and 8in. howitzers.)

Though the production of 9.2in. howitzers was considerable, it was not sufficient to keep up with the anticipated demand for such weapons. Because of this, the British Army ordered the conversion of a number of 6in. coastal defence guns into 8in. siege howitzers. This was largely a matter of cutting down the barrel, reaming out the bore, adjusting the recoil mechanism, and mounting the whole arrangement on a new carriage. Though the weapons that resulted from these conversions were not nearly as powerful as the 9.2in. howitzers, they were surprisingly effective. They were also light enough to be mounted on wheeled carriages, which made them far more mobile than the platform-mounted 9.2in. pieces.

Where more intimate artillery was concerned, the end of 1916 found the Expeditionary Force equipped with a very effective trench mortar. This weapon, the 3in. 'Stokes gun', was a relatively light and remarkably simple means of spitting out relatively sophisticated bombs at a very high rate of fire. At a time when the loading and firing of other trench mortars required several discrete motions – the insertion of a separate propelling charge, the careful fitting of the projectile, the setting of an ignition device and the pulling of a lanyard – the loading and firing of a Stokes mortar was entirely a matter of dropping the bomb into the barrel.

Before the Stokes mortar found its way to the Western Front, the light trench mortar batteries of the Expeditionary Force had to make do with a number of decidedly inferior weapons – the 3.7in. trench mortar, the 4in. smoothbore trench mortar and the 4in. rifled trench mortar. These were, in effect, crude copies of the muzzle-loading artillery pieces of earlier centuries, with modern friction-tubes replacing the simple touchholes of the older pieces and little bags of cordite propellant taking the place of black powder charges. For a variety of reasons, which included the inferior materials from which these weapons were made and the ever-present temptation to use too much propellant, these weapons were plagued by the problem of frequent premature explosions. Because of this, most trench mortar batteries adopted the practice of only pulling the (very long) firing lanyard on such weapons after the crew had taken shelter. As might be imagined, this had the effect of further reducing rates of fire that were already painfully slow.

The weapon of choice of the medium trench mortar batteries of 1916 was the 2in. spigot mortar. Rather than being loaded in the manner of conventional artillery pieces, the spherical 60lb projectile fired by this weapon was mounted on a metal rod. This rod, in turn, was placed inside the rather narrow barrel (the 'spigot') of the mortar. Thus, when the 2in. mortar was fired, the propellant charge acted upon the rod, which then transferred the propulsive forces to the projectile itself. The great advantage of this

Super-heavy guns, like the 12in. naval gun shown here, were of little use in the type of fighting that took place in 1916. Far too inaccurate to be used against German fortifications, they were much more susceptible to barrel wear than smaller weapons. (Library of Congress)

arrangement was the ability to fire a relatively large bomb from a weapon with a relatively small barrel. (The standard projectile fired by the 2in. mortar carried 12lb of explosive, which was the same payload as that of a 5in. howitzer shell.) The drawbacks of the 2in. mortar included a very slow rate of fire, an ostentatious firing signature, very short range and the tendency for the propelling rods to fall on British-held positions. (These deficiencies were shared by the weapon that the 2in. trench mortar replaced in the course of 1916 – the spigot mortar that was variously known as the '1.57in.' and the '1.5in.' trench mortar.)

In routine positional warfare – the situation that arose in the trenches when neither a major offensive nor a widely respected 'trench truce' was in effect – the Stokes mortars of light trench mortar batteries and the 2in. spigot mortars of medium trench mortar batteries had very similar missions. They harassed the enemy, retaliated when the enemy displayed excessive zeal and supported local actions (such as raids and patrols). In a major battle, however, the roles of the two types of trench mortars became very different. Because of their light weight, the rapidity with which they could be set up and the relatively light weight of the bombs they fired, the Stokes mortars could follow the infantry in the attack. Because they were difficult to move and provided with very heavy projectiles, the 2in. spigot mortars could not. Their role in a major battle was to prepare the way for the attackers, primarily by cutting lanes in barbed wire obstacles. To this end, they were increasingly provided with fuses of the instantaneous type. By causing the 'toffee apple' to explode before it could bury itself in the ground, these increased the amount of wire that could be cut while minimizing the creation of craters.

The high quality of most of the weapons issued to the fighting units of the Expeditionary Force was greatly diminished by the low quality of much of the ammunition that they were given to fire. Nearly all of the rifles, machine guns and artillery pieces manufactured during the first two years of the war were produced in factories that had been making weapons for a decade or more. (The newest of the factories engaged in the manufacture of artillery was the Coventry Ordnance Works, which had opened its doors in 1905.) The same, however, was not true of many of the firms engaged to make small-arms ammunition, artillery projectiles, hand grenades, rifle grenades and mortar bombs. Lacking detailed knowledge of the items they were building and under great pressure from the Ministry of Munitions to favour quantity over quality, these firms produced a great deal of defective ammunition.

As a result, British infantrymen on the front lines were often plagued by rifle cartridges that were hard to extract, hand grenades that exploded prematurely (or not at all) and mortar bombs with faulty primers. Gunners found themselves firing a large percentage of duds, loading shells that stripped the lining out of artillery pieces and, what was worst of all, shells that exploded before leaving the barrel of a gun or howitzer.

In the years after the Russo-Japanese War (1904–05), many officers of the Indian Army became very interested in trench warfare. One of the products of this interest was the 'Bangalore torpedo' – an explosive-filled pipe designed to clear lanes in barbed wire obstacles. On the Western Front, these devices proved useful in cases where the wire in question was too close to friendly troops to be dealt with by trench mortars or field artillery. (Royal Engineers Journal)

Tactics

Reduced to its essence, tactics is the art of placing the enemy in a position where his only choice is to submit or die. In other words, tactics is a matter of manoeuvre – the combination of fire, movement and a myriad of psychological effects (surprise, deception, disorientation) to rapidly create a trap around hostile forces. (Where this trap is erected upon enemy-held ground, the tactics are offensive. Where this trap is built on one's own territory, the tactics are defensive. In either case, tactics are largely a matter of putting the enemy in a position of 'damned if you do and damned if you don't'.)

For the original Expeditionary Force, the small field army that was formed in 1907 and deployed to France at the start of World War I, tactics was largely the work of formations – divisions, groups of divisions and the Expeditionary Force itself. Within divisions, units of rifle-armed infantry and shrapnel-firing field artillery rarely created traps of their own. Instead, they practised a branch of the art of war that the leading military thinkers of the day characterized as 'battle technique'. That is, their actions – which combined fire, movement, direct assaults and the occupation of ground – provided the elements that the generals commanding formations could use to engineer dilemmas on a considerably larger scale. (The classic form for these dilemmas was the envelopment, which placed the enemy between two powerful forces and thus deprived him of the ability to concentrate his forces against one without exposing himself to the other.) In other words, units acted in a frontal, linear fashion so that formations could manoeuvre in a concentric, non-linear manner.

As early as the winter of 1915, German units on the Western Front had begun to dig deep shelters of various sorts. These shelters, which were much more resistant to the effects of heavy howitzer shells than conventional trenches, would play an important role in the battles of 1916. (Library of Congress)

By 1916, this neat division of labour was being torn asunder by two very powerful forces. The first of these was the downward expansion of the realm of tactics. The second of these was the upward expansion of the realm of technique. To be more precise, the widespread availability of trench mortars, hand grenades and light machine guns reduced the echelon at which units were able to manoeuvre in a concentric, non-linear fashion while the proliferation of long-range artillery pieces allowed infantry divisions and army corps to act in a manner that had once been restricted to lower echelons – to act solely by fire, to directly coordinate fire and movement, and to carry out assaults.

The simultaneous expansion of the previously separate realms of 'tactics' and 'battle technique' pulled the Expeditionary Force in two very different directions. Tactics required an approach to command that was highly decentralized, one that depended heavily upon the initiative of leaders and consequently gave them a great deal of latitude. Technique required centralized control – punctual adherence to scripts and timetables rather than improvisation or creativity. Thus was born one of the great paradoxes of the middle years of World War I. The Expeditionary Force that had gone to war in 1914 was the beneficiary of a long tradition of 'trusting the man on the spot'. In such areas as trench raids – which might well be described as 'battles in miniature' – this tradition provided a solid foundation for excellent small-unit tactics. When it came to operations carried out on a larger scale, the rise of formation-level battle technique eclipsed this tradition, thereby depriving many units of the freedom they needed to exploit fleeting opportunities.

Combat operations

From the point of view of British offensive operations, the second year of World War I began on 10 May 1915, the day that Sir John French decided to end the battle of Aubers Ridge. An important part of this decision was the realization that the methods that had previously governed major British offensives during the first year of the war – the intense 'hurricane' bombardment of German forward positions and the attempt to break through the entire German defensive system in a single bound – were no longer a suitable response to the situation at hand. Where bombardments were concerned, the Expeditionary Force lacked the ammunition needed to conduct hurricane bombardments that were strong enough to completely destroy the type of front-line defences the Germans were building at the time. In terms of the uninterrupted breakthrough, the experience of the battle of Neuve Chapelle (9–13 March 1915) had demonstrated that the Germans could plug a gap torn in their lines faster than the British could exploit it.

The most readily available alternative to hurricane bombardment was a technique that was already being used by the French Army – the methodical bombardment. Where the hurricane bombardment required all participating artillery pieces to fire nearly as fast as they could for a period of less than an hour, the methodical bombardment called for the guns and howitzers of the attacking force to fire at a very slow rate over the course of several days and nights. This permitted careful observation of the strike of every round, frequent evaluation of the damage inflicted on particular targets and the tailoring of the latter phases of the bombardment to the actual condition of the defences being attacked. The expenditure of precious shells upon targets that had already been destroyed was thus avoided and the waste resulting from inaccurate fire was greatly reduced. This, in turn, meant that a given stretch of trench could be thoroughly bombarded at a much lower cost in propellant and projectiles.

Table 21: Employment of siege howitzers in preparatory bombardments

	Neuve Chapelle, 10 March 1915	Aubers Ridge, 9 May 1915	Festubert, 15 May 1915	Loos, 25 September 1915	Somme, 1 July 1916
6in. howitzer	24	36	36	36	104
8in. howitzer	0	0	0	16	64
9.2in. howitzer	3	9	9	12	116
12in. howitzer	0	0	0	0	11
Total howitzers	27	45	45	54	295
Frontage (yards)	1,350	3,000	5,000	11,200	25,000
Yards per howitzer	54	67	111	207	85

Table 22: Rounds fired by 6in. howitzers in preparatory bombardments

	Neuve Chapelle, 10 March 1915	Aubers Ridge, 9 May 1915	Festubert, 15 May 1915	Loos, 25 September 1915	Somme, 1 July 1916
6in. howitzer Shells	3,364	3,767	2,848	11,241	83,200
Frontage (yards)	1,350	3,000	5,000	11,200	25,000
Shells per yard	2.49	1.25	0.56	1.00	3.32

Calibre	4.5in.	6in.	8in.	9.2in.	12in.
Table 23: Accumulation of high-explosive howitzer shells by the Expeditionary Force, June 1915–June 1916					
1 June 1915	1,182	100	220	859	0
1 December 1915	62,897	19,075	12,031	6,087	2,208
1 June 1916	481,472	143,409	32,015	37,182	6,991

The great defect of methodical bombardment was that it telegraphed British intentions to the Germans, giving them ample warning of an impending attack as well as significant information about the location, scale and extent of the initial assault. It thus allowed the Germans to reinforce local reserves, to bring up additional supplies, to finalize preparations for the containment of the attacking force, to custom-tailor arrangements for counterattacks and to make provision for the eventual rebuilding of the defences being destroyed. In short, the methodical battle sacrificed the advantages of surprise and shock effect on the altar of economy and efficiency.

Festubert

The first British offensive to be preceded by a methodical bombardment was, like the first two big offensive operations of 1915, aimed at the capture of Aubers Ridge. Named for the nearby village of Festubert, this attack was actually a long series of relatively small attacks carried out over the course of a fortnight (15–27 May 1915).

The bombardments that preceded the first two of these attacks lasted for 60 hours. For three successive days, 18-pdrs fired shrapnel shells against the German barbed wire, with the effect of every round upon the wire obstacles being observed before the next round was fired. Simultaneously, howitzers of various sizes (4.5in., 5in., 6in., 9.2in. and 15in.) attempted the methodical destruction of parapets, trenches, strongpoints and villages while heavy guns (4.7in., 60-pdr and 6in.) tried to destroy German artillery pieces that had been identified by observers in the air. At night, field guns of various sorts fired shrapnel shells at places where such fire might interfere with German efforts to bring up supplies, repair their wire or reinforce their forward garrisons.

Many of the shells fired during the battle of the Somme were aimed at dummy batteries. Though these were often crudely built, they were good enough to deceive observers viewing them from a distance of several 1,000 yards and soldiers examining aerial photographs. (Author's Collection)

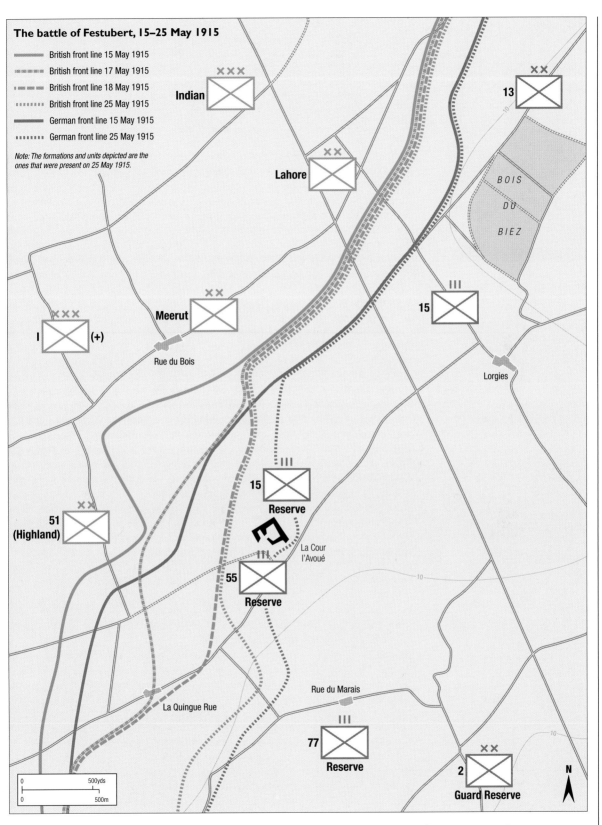

The battle of Festubert, 15–25 May 1915

British front line 15 May 1915
British front line 17 May 1915
British front line 18 May 1915
British front line 25 May 1915
German front line 15 May 1915
German front line 25 May 1915

Note: The formations and units depicted are the ones that were present on 25 May 1915.

Indian

Lahore

13

BOIS
DU
BIEZ

Meerut

15

I (+)

Rue du Bois

Lorgies

51 (Highland)

15
Reserve

La Cour l'Avoué

55
Reserve

77
Reserve

Rue du Marais

La Quingue Rue

2
Guard Reserve

N

0 ____ 500yds
0 ____ 500m

Though overall supervision of the operation rested with corps headquarters, individual infantry brigades, or pairs of infantry brigades, carried out the many attacks that made up the battle of Festubert.

Many of the British shells fired during the middle years of the war failed to explode. These three 'duds' – from a 15in. howitzer, an 8in. howitzer and a 60-pdr heavy gun – were recovered after the battle of Loos. (Author's Collection)

Of these four efforts, only the wire cutting had any significant effect on the German defences. The fuses on many howitzer shells failed to work, the counter-battery fire failed to do much permanent damage to the German artillery and the harassing fire was insufficiently dense to keep the Germans from making their own preparations for the battle. Because of this, only three of the five British brigades attacking on the first day of the battle managed to capture the sections of the German forward position that had served as their initial objectives. Two of these brigades (the 20th and 22nd Brigades of the 7th Division) owed much of their success to the work of six field guns that had been employed as direct-fire 'infantry guns' during the last phase of the bombardment. Firing high-explosive shells over open sights, these six guns (four 18-pdrs and two 13-pdrs) were able to inflict a great deal of damage upon nearby German parapets.

The net effect of the five British attacks was to create two penetrations in the German forward line – one to the north of a German strongpoint known as the 'Quadrilateral' and one to the south. In the course of the second day of the operation (16 May), small parties of British infantry used hand grenades to reduce the length of this position. Thus, nightfall found the German defenders in the awkward position of being in a small position that, in addition to being nearly surrounded by British troops, was within range of a substantial number of British howitzers.

Early in the morning of the third day of the battle (17 May), 33 of these howitzers (30 4.5in. field howitzers and three 9.2in. siege howitzers) subjected the German-held areas in the vicinity of the Quadrilateral to a methodical bombardment. Thanks to the careful registration of these pieces in the course of the preparatory bombardment, the fire concentrated upon the German position was extraordinarily accurate. By 0700hrs, white flags had begun to appear on the German parapet and hundreds of German soldiers were making their way towards the British-held trenches in the hope of being able to surrender. (Many of these would-be prisoners of war were killed while running across the intervening ground, either by German shells aimed at suspected British positions, or by the fire of British gunners who did not realize that the Germans were unarmed.)

While the bombardment of the Quadrilateral was taking place, the Germans were hard at work bringing up reinforcements and establishing a new defensive position. Thus, even though the remaining defenders of the Quadrilateral offered little resistance to the British battalions sent forward to occupy it, the fourth day of the battle (18 May) found most German units in the vicinity of Festubert well protected by carefully sited trenches and stoutly built parapets. To make matters worse, the supply of ammunition for the 4.5in. and 6in. howitzers that had inflicted so much damage upon the Quadrilateral had been exhausted. Thus any subsequent bombardments would be conducted by weapons ill suited to the task at hand.

On the afternoon of 18 May, two fresh infantry brigades – the 3rd Canadian Brigade (of the Canadian Division) and the 4th (Guards) Brigade (of the 2nd Division) – conducted attacks that, even by the standards of Western Front, were extraordinarily confused affairs. Both attacks, which were scheduled to begin at 1630hrs, were preceded by a two-hour bombardment. However, as none of the officers giving the orders for the operation were aware that the Germans had pulled back all of their forward units to their new line of resistance, the shells fell along a line ran that several hundred yards in front of the actual German positions.

Additional confusion was caused by the time that it took for officers at each echelon of command to issue the necessary orders for the operation. The decision to conduct these attacks was taken personally by Sir Douglas Haig, the general officer commanding the First Army, at 1355hrs. Despite the reliable telephone connections between all of the headquarters involved, it took 50 minutes to get division orders to both of the infantry brigades making the attack, more than an hour to inform all of the artillery batteries of their targets, and nearly two hours to provide each infantry battalion with its instructions. Because of this, the artillery bombardment was 30 minutes behind schedule and one of the infantry brigades (the 3rd Canadian Brigade) did not reach its jumping off trenches until 1720hrs and the other brigade told off for the attack – the 4th (Guards) Brigade of the 2nd Division – attacked alone. Before they had crossed the first 100 yards (90m) of the half-mile or so (800m) that separated them from their objectives, the four forward companies of the 4th Brigade lost half of their men to German machine-gun fire. Seeing this, the brigade commander quickly realized that, even if some of his men managed to reach the German trenches, they would be too weak to take them. He therefore stopped the attack, telling his men to consolidate their hold on the bit of ground they had taken.

The last two attacks of the battle of Festubert had much in common with those of 18 May. On 24 May, an attack by two brigades – the 140th Brigade of the 47th (2nd London) Division and the 2nd Canadian Brigade – managed a modest advance, taking a small position sticking out of the German forward line. On 25 May, the 142nd Brigade, also of the 47th Division, gained ground to a depth of some 400 yards (360m) before it was stopped by German artillery fire.

For the leaders of the Expeditionary Force, the chief lesson of the battle of Festubert was the same as the chief lesson of the battles of Neuve Chapelle (10–13 March 1915) and Aubers Ridge (9 May 1915): the indispensable pre-requisites for a successful attack in position warfare were effective wire cutting and the dropping of a large number of howitzer shells (whether 4.5in. or 6in.) on each German trench to be taken. Slowing down the pace of bombardment helped to economize on the shells employed for these purposes, but only at the margin.

The Germans drew the same lessons. Having been on the receiving end of one very effective bombardment (at Neuve Chapelle), one completely ineffective bombardment (at Aubers Ridge) and a variety of bombardments of various degrees of effectiveness (in the course of the battle of Festubert), they knew how dangerous the right sort of bombardment could be. They also knew that, once it received a sufficient number of howitzer shells, 4.5in. howitzers and 6in. howitzers with on-carriage recoil mechanisms, the Expeditionary Force could demolish, at will, substantial portions of the German front line. They therefore set to work on building a series of reserve positions.

When trench warfare started, most of the German positions were sited on forward slopes. This ensured that, should they choose to attack, their enemies would be attacking up hill. It also gave a good field of fire to German rifles and machine guns. The Achilles heel of a forward slope position, however, was its vulnerability to artillery fire. With trenches and strongpoints in full view of hostile artillery observers, enemy batteries could zero in on their targets with relative ease and, as long as sufficient shells were available, demolish them in a matter of hours. Because of this, the Germans knew that, as soon as their enemies acquired a sufficient stock of the right sort of artillery, any given forward position could only resist attack for a short period of time.

The reserve positions, which were located two miles or so behind the forward positions, were designed on a different principle. Rather than being placed on a forward slope, they were placed on a rear slope, with the forward line of trenches some 200 yards below the crest. This meant that, in order to bring effective artillery fire to bear, an attacker would have to place his observers along a ridge that was not only within 200 yards or so of a trench that was full of German riflemen and machine-gunners, but also subject to an enormous amount of German artillery fire. The cost of gaining this advantage, moreover, was a relatively small one, for most of the damage done by German small arms (whether rifles or machine guns) was inflicted at ranges of 200 yards or less.

While some shells failed to explode at all, others exploded too soon. When such premature explosions took place within the barrel of an artillery piece, the result was often fatal for members of the gun crew. (Author's collection)

At the end of the battle of Festubert, Sir John French had made it clear to his superiors in London that the Expeditionary Force could not conduct any more attacks until it had built up a substantial reserve of artillery ammunition. As this would require the better part of a year, he expected to refrain from ordering any major attacks for quite some time. At the same time, French permitted three offensive enterprises that were aimed at strictly local objectives – attacks by pairs of infantry brigades that were designed to wrest relatively small pieces of key terrain away from the Germans.

The manner in which these attacks were prepared varied greatly from one to the other. The attack at Givenchy, south of Neuve Chapelle, was preceded by a 48-hour bombardment in the style of the battle of Festubert. The attack at Bellewaarde Ridge, near Ypres, followed a modified 'hurricane' bombardment (lasting 105 minutes) and the blowing of a small mine. The attack at Hooge, also near Ypres, exploited the explosion of a large mine. Notwithstanding these differences, the results of the attacks were essentially the same. The attacking brigades succeeded in breaking into the German forward position and, in most places, made short work of the first German trench they encountered. Beyond the first trench, however, they ran into heavy resistance from the garrisons of the German support trench, small groups armed with hand grenades and well-sited machine guns. Unable to move forward, the attacking brigades lost a large number of men to German artillery fire.

Loos

During the summer of 1915, while the Expeditionary Force was still in the midst of its shell crisis, the French Army had managed to built up a respectable reserve of artillery ammunition. General Joseph Joffre, in command of all of the French armies on the Western Front, planned to use these shells in a grand, double-pronged offensive that he had scheduled for the end of September. At first, Sir John French declined Joffre's request that the Expeditionary Force conduct a parallel offensive of its own. He could not, however, decline a similar request from Lord Kitchener. (As had been the case for more than a year, Kitchener was worried about the situation on the Eastern Front. He therefore endorsed the French offensive as a means of keeping the Germans from devoting all of their energies to the defeat of Russia.)

The area chosen for the new British offensive was a stretch of mining country that began at the town of La Bassée and ran south, for seven miles or so, to the town of Lens. In contrast to the flat ground near Ypres and the

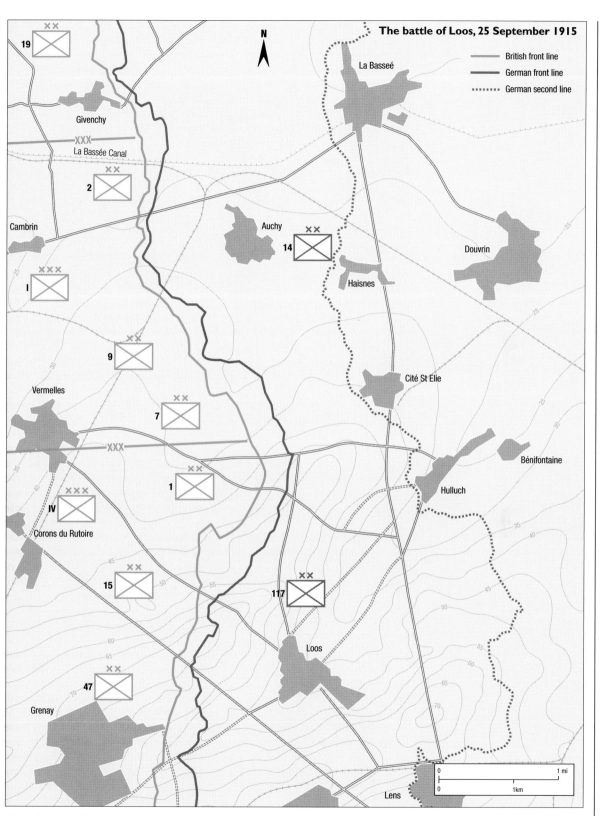

The battle of Loos, 25 September 1915

British front line
German front line
German second line

19
2
Givenchy
La Bassée Canal
Cambrin
I
9
Vermelles
7
1
IV
Corons du Rutoire
15
47
Grenay

La Basseé
Auchy
14
Douvrin
Haisnes
Cité St Elie
Bénifontaine
Hulluch
117
Loos
Lens

0   1 mi
0   1km

The techniques refined during the battle of Festubert worked well against the German forward position, most of which was located on forward slopes. They were much less effective against the second German position, which made much better use of the highly irregular terrain of the Loos battlefield.

smooth, gentle slope leading up to Aubers Ridge, the terrain on this battlefield was highly irregular, with lots of odd-shaped ridges, unexpected valleys and little settlements. It was thus well suited for the new German defensive scheme, which made extensive use of rear-slope reserve positions and hidden machine-gun nests.

The task of conducting the offensive, which was soon given the name of Loos (after a village just north of Lens), was assigned to Sir Douglas Haig, the general officer commanding the First Army. Haig's plan called for the simultaneous advance of six infantry divisions. As these six divisions would form a line that was nearly 12,000 yards long, the preliminary bombardment could not be as fierce as it had been at the battle of Neuve Chapelle. Rather, with only one and a half siege howitzer shells (whether 6, 8 or 9.2in.) falling for each yard of the line to be attacked, the preliminary bombardment would only be as dense as the one the preceded the first attack of the battle of Festubert. Because of this, Haig decided to top off his preliminary bombardment with a cloud of chlorine gas.

Under the right conditions, chlorine gas would have been a very effective means of economizing upon artillery shells. Because it was heavier than air, it tended to sink into the dugouts and cellars where German soldiers took shelter in the course of a bombardment. A cloud of chlorine gas, however, was also completely dependent upon the wind. If the wind failed to blow in the desired direction, there was no sense in releasing the cloud. If the wind changed direction, the cloud would end up in the wrong place. Much of the German reserve position, moreover, was located on ground that was higher than the British front line. Because of this, the gas would have little effect upon the most dangerous feature of the German defensive system.

On 25 September 1915, the day of the attack, much of the gas cloud failed to move in the desired direction. In the northern half of the battlefield, the gas cloud stood still, blocking the path of most of the battalions leading the attack of I Corps (2nd, 9th and 7th Divisions) and causing many casualties. Further south, in the sector of IV Corps, only one division (1st Division) had to deal with substantial interference from 'friendly' gas. The other two (15th and 47th Divisions) made considerable progress, breaking through the German front line and taking the village of Loos in a matter of hours. By mid-morning, the leading elements of 15th Division had reached the top of Hill 70, a feature that sheltered a portion of the German reserve position.

While some of the companies on top of Hill 70 set about consolidating their position, others pressed forward, moving down the eastern slope of the hill until they reached the wire in front of the German reserve position. There they came under fire from three directions – bullets fired by rifles and machine guns and shells fired by artillery pieces. For three hours, 900 British soldiers

In the early days of trench warfare, German barbed-wire obstacles were made of relatively thin wire that could be cut to ribbons by a relatively small number of well-aimed (and properly fused) 18-pdr shrapnel shells. By the middle of 1915, however, the Germans had started to use a thicker grade of wire that was much more resistant to this sort of treatment. (Great War in a Different Light)

Though the infantry was to follow in the wake of the gas cloud (rather than through it), this drawing does a good job of depicting the gas 'helmets' issued to British troops prior to the battle of Loos. (Great War in a Different Light)

lay under this fire, unable to move in any direction. At 1300hrs, the Germans counterattacked, sweeping up the small number of men who had not been killed or wounded, and recapturing Hill 70.

On the second day of the battle, 26 September 1915, General Haig sent in the two divisions he had been keeping in reserve – the 21st and 24th Divisions of XI Corps. These advanced across a large depression north of the village of Loos, against a portion of the German reserve position that had been built on top of a crescent-shaped ridge. Unfortunately, the batteries that were to bombard the German trenches prior to this attack had taken up the wrong positions. As a result, the preliminary bombardment of the German reserve position was limited to a handful of ranging shots. However, as the order to advance had not been cancelled, the ten battalions told off to lead the attack stepped off at the appointed time, 1100hrs.

As they advanced, the ten lead battalions – some 10,000 officers and men – came under the fire of eight infantry companies, a dozen or so machine guns and a battery of six 77mm field guns. Displaying magnificent discipline, the attacking battalions maintained their formations and, though dozens of men fell with every minute that passed, continued to march across the mile of open ground that separated them from the German position. By the time that these units reached the German wire, they had lost nearly all of their officers and more than three-quarters of their men. Realizing that the German wire was still intact, the lead battalions began to retire.

The battle continued for three more weeks, with periods of relative calm alternating with local attacks. When, on 13 October 1915, the British offensive was officially brought to an end, the bulk of the original reserve position was still in German hands. For the Expeditionary Force, the price of taking the ground in front of that position was nearly 43,000 officers and men – 16,000 of whom had been killed and the rest either taken prisoner or badly wounded. For the German Army, the cost of holding on to the reserve position was the loss (by death, serious wounds or capture) of 21,000 or so officers and men.

The Somme

In the nine months that passed between the end of the battle of Loos (13 October 1915) and the beginning of the battles of the Somme (1 July 1916), the Expeditionary Force accumulated an enormous amount of artillery ammunition. Had the development of German defensive tactics stood still, this great horde of shells would have allowed the application, on a much larger scale, of the tactics that had worked so well on the first day of the battle of Neuve Chapelle. As might

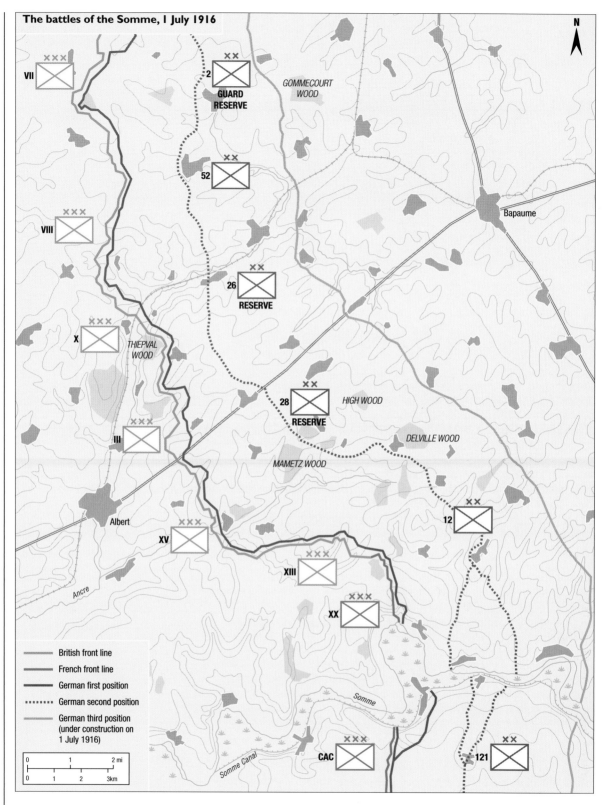

The battles of the Somme, 1 July 1916

N

VII

2
GUARD
RESERVE

GOMMECOURT
WOOD

52

VIII

Bapaume

26
RESERVE

X

THIEPVAL
WOOD

28
RESERVE

HIGH WOOD

III

DELVILLE WOOD

MAMETZ WOOD

12

Albert

XV

XIII

XX

Ancre

British front line
French front line
German first position
German second position
German third position
(under construction on
1 July 1916)

0   1   2 mi
0   1   2   3km

Somme

Somme Canal

CAC

121

Though the Somme battlefield was dotted with villages, many of the fiercest combats took place in woods and copses. The chief reason for this was the effect that the thick summer foliage had upon aerial observation. While British observers could spot German positions in villages with relative ease, they could not see past the treetops of heavily wooded areas.

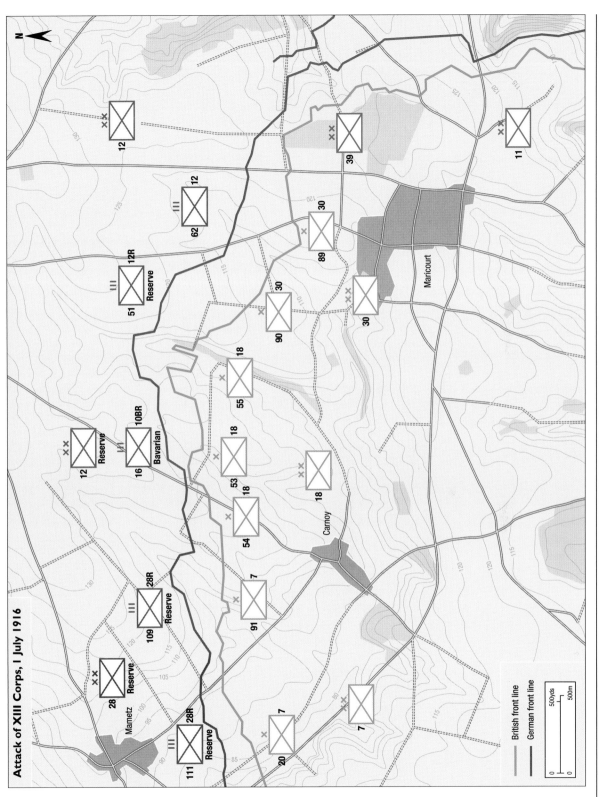

Attack of XIII Corps, 1 July 1916

12

12
III
62

12R
III
Reserve
51

39

30
89

30
90

30
30

Maricourt

18
55

18
53
18
54

18
18

12
II
Reserve
10BR
16
Bavarian

28R
III
109
Reserve

7
91

28
II
Reserve
Mametz

28R
III
111
Reserve

7
7

20

Carnoy

British front line
German front line

500yds
0
500m
0

The most successful of the many British attacks on the first day of the battles of the Somme was that of XIII Corps. One reason for this success was the location of the German first position, which lay along an exposed forward slope. Another was the assistance provided by the French heavy artillery. Composed mostly of long-range guns, this artillery was well suited to the task of bombarding a forward slope. A third reason was the absence of heavily wooded areas on the German side of no-man's land.

While there were a few instances during the battle of the Somme where German infantry units employed their rifles to good effect, the chief weapons of the defenders of German positions were hand grenades and machine guns. (Author's collection)

be expected, however, the Germans had learned much from the many defensive battles they had fought in 1915. In particular, they had greatly increased the depth of their defences, building two additional positions behind their forward positions. They had increased the distance between the two or three trench lines within each position and provided those trenches with well-built underground shelters. They had built a number of supplementary works (such as machine-gun nests) in the space between positions. Worst of all, they had not only increased the extent of their barbed-wire obstacles, they had also begun to use much thicker grades of wire.

The preliminary bombardment began on the morning of 24 June 1916, with the systematic shelling of barbed-wire obstacles and a programme of counter-battery fire. Two days later, the attempt to destroy fortified positions – the trenches, strongpoints and machine-gun nests that sheltered the German infantry – began in earnest. Later that afternoon, a set of aerial photographs made it clear that the wire-cutting was not proceeding as expected. Thus, the trench mortars and howitzers that had previously done the bulk of the wire-cutting work were reinforced by large numbers of 18-pdrs. Even so, patrols sent out in the intervals between programmes of fire often reported that much of the wire in front of German positions was still intact.

On 28 June, General Haig delayed the start of the infantry attack for two complete days. Thus, rather than ending on the morning of 29 June, the preliminary bombardment was to last until 0730hrs on 1 July. This decision, which was prompted by the request of the general commanding the French forces taking part in the offensive, gave the British artillery 48 additional hours to finish cutting the German wire. Unfortunately, the ammunition needed to make the most of the additional time was not available. As a result, the last phase of the bombardment was much less intense than it would have been otherwise.

The effects achieved by the preliminary bombardment varied greatly from one part of the battlefield to another. In some places, the wire was cleared away, the German artillery effectively silenced and the German forward position smashed to pieces. (This was particularly true for the two army corps closest to the river Somme, XIII Corps of the Expeditionary Force and the 20ème Corps d'Armée of the French Army.) In other places, one or more of the key features of the German defensive array – the wire, the forward position or the artillery – remained intact. As might be expected, the attacking infantry made the greatest progress where

A significant number of French units took part in the battle of the Somme. In this picture, one of the few Rimailho howitzers still in service with the French Army in 1916 fires in support of the 20ème Corps d'Armée. (Author's collection)

the bombardment had been most successful. Even those divisions that managed to take all of their objectives, however, suffered heavy losses.

In the two weeks that followed the first day of the offensive, a series of smaller operations finished the task of capturing the German forward position. On 11 July, the artillery of three army corps began a systematic bombardment of the German reserve position. Three days later, at dawn on 14 July, six infantry brigades attacked Longueval Ridge, a piece of high ground that was home to a four-mile section of that position. Thanks to very careful preparation, the combined effects of a number of small innovations, and the fact that most of this position was located on a forward slope, this attack was a complete success. The attempt to exploit this victory, however, did not go so well. Once they had passed over the crest of Longueval Ridge, the British units sent forward for this purpose found themselves involved in a new type of positional warfare, one in which the struggle for control of well-defined positions had been replaced by house-to-house fighting in ruined villages and close-quarters combat in wooded areas.

During the four months that followed, the pattern set by the first month of the battles of Somme would be repeated many times. Prepared attacks of the type carried out on the first day of the offensive would alternate with long struggles for control of woods and villages. The human cost of these battles was enormous, with more than a million men (some 400,000 from the Expeditionary Force, 200,000 from the French Army and 400,000 from the German Army) suffering death or serious wounds. The chief purpose of the great offensive, however, had been achieved. The Germans were effectively deprived of forces that might otherwise have inflicted serious, war-winning defeats on France and Russia.

As the commander of IV Corps, Sir Henry Rawlinson (1864–1925) had played a key role in all of the offensives undertaken by the Expeditionary Force in 1915. As the commander of the Fourth Army, he was in charge of all British forces directly involved in the Somme offensive. (Library of Congress)

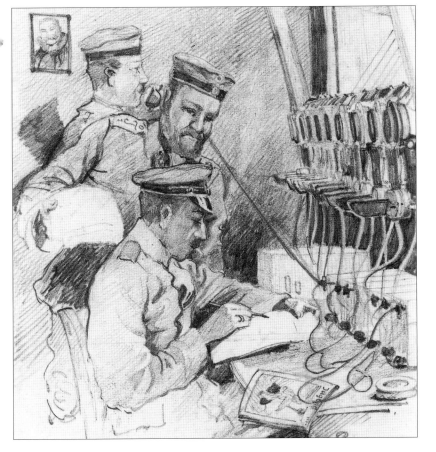

The German defensive tactics employed at the Somme were heavily dependent upon underground telephone exchanges, which relayed messages from well-placed observers to well-hidden artillery batteries. (Library of Congress)

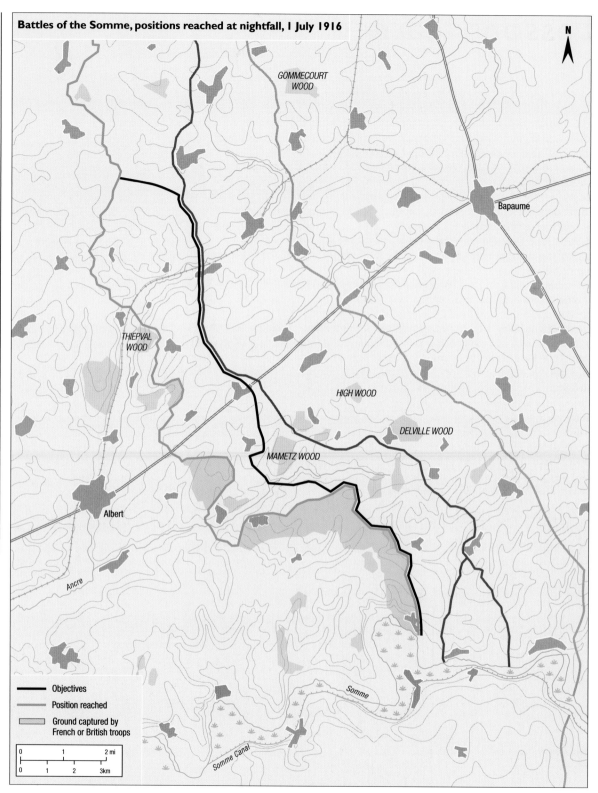

Battles of the Somme, positions reached at nightfall, 1 July 1916

N

GOMMECOURT WOOD

Bapaume

THIEPVAL WOOD

HIGH WOOD

DELVILLE WOOD

MAMETZ WOOD

Albert

Ancre

Somme

Somme Canal

Objectives

Position reached

Ground captured by
French or British troops

| 0 | | 1 | | 2 mi |
| 0 | 1 | | 2 | 3km |

The lion's share of the progress made by French and British forces on the first day of the battles of the Somme took place on the southern end of the battlefield, in the zones of attack assigned to the British XIII Corps and the French 20ème Corps d'Armée. Many historians attribute this success to the ferocity of the French preliminary bombardment, which employed far more heavy pieces per yard of front than the British bombardment.

Lessons learned

The chief lesson learned by the Expeditionary Force in the course of 1916 – and, in particular, during the five long months of the Somme offensive – was that the lessons of 1915 no longer applied. In the course of 1915, British soldiers fighting on the Western Front had come to the conclusion that the chief prerequisite for a successful attack was a preliminary bombardment that destroyed all things capable of inflicting harm or delay upon the attackers. By the end of 1916, it was clear that, except for barbed-wire obstacles, the deadliest features of a German defensive array were no longer subject to complete destruction. That is to say, no matter how numerous or heavy British shells might be, a certain number of German soldiers would emerge from the wreckage of their positions with both the will to fight and the means of inflicting considerable losses upon the attackers.

The solution to this conundrum was to replace the simple notion of artillery destroying all in the path of attacking infantry with a much more sophisticated view of the effects created by various forms of artillery fire. In particular, British soldiers came to the conclusion that the temporary effects of various kinds of artillery fire were often more important than the permanent ones, that the killing of a few enemy soldiers had less impact upon the course of a battle than the short-term paralysis of many. The chief product of this change in thinking was the 'creeping barrage' – a thick belt of high-explosive shells that 'crept' forward at the pace of a walking man. In situations where the attacking infantry was able to keep pace with this barrage, the defenders of a given position would be forced to remain in their shelters until the moment when the attacking infantry was upon them. Thus, rather than facing well-hidden machine guns at a range of 200 yards, British infantrymen would, if all went well, catch machine-gun crews before they had a chance to set up their weapons.

Tanks made their battlefield debut in September 1916. They would not, however, play a decisive role in any battle fought on the Western Front until the autumn of 1917. (Author's collection)

Chronology

1915

1 May	The German Ninth Army attacks Russian positions in southern Poland, thereby beginning the battle of Gorlice-Tarnow.
3 May	The battle of Gorlice-Tarnow ends with an unambiguous victory for the Central Powers.
4 May	The Germans and Austro-Hungarians exploit their victory at Gorlice-Tarnow by beginning their conquest of Russian-occupied Poland.
4 May	The French Tenth Army begins the artillery preparation for its attack in Artois.
7 May	A German submarine sinks the British passenger ship *Lusitania* off the coast of Ireland. More than any other single event, this action turns public opinion in the United States against Germany.
9 May	The French Tenth Army launches its attack in Artois.
9 May	The battle of Aubers Ridge begins. It is aimed at both the capture of Aubers Ridge and the drawing off of German forces that might otherwise be used against the French or Russians.
10 May	The battle of Aubers Ridge ends in a clear defeat for the British attackers.
15 May	The battle of Festubert begins.
23 May	Italy enters World War I by declaring war on Austria-Hungary.
25 May	The Germans call off their attack at Ypres.
27 May	Sir John French calls off the attack at Festubert, announcing that the Expeditionary Force must cease all offensive operations until the shortage of artillery ammunition is solved.
22 June	German and Austro-Hungarian forces recapture Lemberg (present-day Lviv), the capital of the Austro-Hungarian province of Galicia.
3 October	French and British forces land at Salonika, thereby establishing the Macedonian Front.
18 December	British Empire troops begin to evacuate their positions on the Gallipoli Peninsula.
19 December	Sir Douglas Haig replaces Sir John French as commander-in-chief of the Expeditionary Force.

1916

8 January	British Empire troops complete their withdrawal from the Gallipoli Peninsula, thereby ending the Gallipoli campaign.
10 February	The Military Service Act, which authorizes conscription, becomes law in the United Kingdom.
21 February	The German Army begins its attack at Verdun.
12 March	An inter-Allied conference at Chantilly decides upon a massive summer offensive. This will become the battles of the Somme.
24 April	The short-lived Easter Rebellion begins in Ireland.
1 May	The Easter Rebellion ends.
25 May	The number of men subject to conscription in the United Kingdom is increased by a second Military Service Act. Among other things, this second law eliminates the automatic exemption of married men.
31 May	The largest single naval engagement of the war, the battle of Jutland, takes place in the North Sea.
4 June	The 'Brusilov Offensive', a massive Russian attack against Austro-Hungarian forces, begins.

5 June	Lord Kitchener, Secretary of State for War, dies at sea.
7 June	David Lloyd George becomes Secretary of State for War.
1 July	The battles of the Somme begin with the start of the battle of Albert.
5 July	4.5in. howitzers of the 30th Division fire 500 thermite shells in an unsuccessful attempt to set fire to Bernafay Wood (battles of the Somme). This is the first use of thermite projectiles in war.
11 July	The German forces at Verdun go on the defensive.
13 July	The battle of Albert ends.
14 July	The battle of Bazentin Ridge (battles of the Somme) begins with the taking of Longueval Ridge.
15 July	The battle of Delville Wood (battles of the Somme) begins.
17 July	The battle of Bazentin Ridge ends.
23 July	The battle of Pozières Ridge (battles of the Somme) begins.
1 August	The German forces at Verdun launch their last attack (at Souville).
7 August	The French begin their attack against the village of Maurepas (battles of the Somme).
24 August	The French take the village of Maurepas (battles of the Somme).
2 September	German and Bulgarian forces invade Romania.
3 September	The battle of Delville Wood (battles of the Somme) ends.
3 September	The battle of Pozières Ridge (battles of the Somme) ends.
3 September	The battle of Guillemont (battles of the Somme) begins.
6 September	The battle of Guillemont (battles of the Somme) ends.
9 September	The battle of Ginchy (battles of the Somme) begins and ends.
15 September	The battle of Flers-Courcelette (battles of the Somme) begins.
22 September	The battle of Flers-Courcelette (battles of the Somme) ends.
23 September	German airships bomb London.
25 September	Battle of Morval (battles of the Somme) begins.
26 September	Battle of Thiepval Ridge (battles of the Somme) begins.
28 September	Battle of Thiepval Ridge (battles of the Somme) ends.
28 September	Battle of Morval (battles of the Somme) ends.
1 October	Battle of the Transloy Ridges (battles of the Somme) begins.
1 October	Battle of the Ancre Heights (battles of the Somme) begins.
18 October	Battle of the Transloy Ridges (battles of the Somme) ends.
11 November	Battle of the Ancre Heights (battles of the Somme) ends.
13 November	Battle of the Ancre (battles of the Somme) begins.
18 November	Battle of the Ancre (battles of the Somme) ends.
18 November	The battles of the Somme end.
19 November	Allied forces in Macedonia take Monastir.
23 November	Greece declares war on Germany.
27 November	German airships attack the eastern coast of England.
28 November	German aeroplanes attack London.
6 December	German forces capture Bucharest.
7 December	David Lloyd George becomes prime minister.
18 December	The battle of Verdun ends.

Further reading

The two relevant volumes of the *Official History of the War (Military Operations, France and Belgium, 1916)* remain the only indispensable works on the achievements of Expeditionary Force in 1916. Unfortunately, the series did not expand at the same rate as the Expeditionary Force itself. (The volumes for 1914 provide a detailed account of the actions of fewer than 15 divisions over a period of five months. The volumes for 1916 contain no more words than those for 1914, but must explain the actions of 60-odd divisions over the course of 12 very busy months.)

The solution to this problem of scale is to consult the many divisional histories that were published soon after the war. These provide information on the middle years of the war that cannot be found anywhere else. Among many other things, they provide invaluable details on those organizational 'orphans' – units such as cyclist companies and trench mortar batteries – that were often ignored by the writers of regimental histories.

Those interested in a soldier's-eye view of battle in 1916 need look no further than Martin Middlebrook's *First Day on the Somme* (Barnsley: Leo Cooper, 2002). This work, which was based on in-depth interviews with veterans, does a first-class job of placing first-hand information in its proper context. Readers looking for a more global perspective – one that attempts to make sense of the inner workings of the Expeditionary Force – will do well to consult Martin Samuels' *Command or Control?* (London: Frank Cass, 1995). Written by an historian with an in-depth understanding of the problems faced by large bureaucracies, Samuels helps the reader go beyond the personality-based debates about the leadership of the Expeditionary Force that, over the years, have generated more heat than light.

Index